The American Fisherman's Fresh and Salt Water Guide

The American Fisherman's
FRESH and SALT
WATER GUIDE

EDITED BY VIN T. SPARANO

WINCHESTER PRESS

To My Mother and Father

Acknowledgments:

"The Natural Baits in Fresh and Salt Water": portions of copyrighted text and photographs reprinted from *Outdoor Life* with permission, 1974 and 1975, Times Mirror Magazines, Inc.

"Don't Spoil Your Fish," and "Knots for the Fisherman": portions of copyrighted text and photographs reprinted from *Outdoor Life* with permission, 1974, Times Mirror Magazines, Inc.

Library of Congress Catalog Card Number: 75–37572
ISBN: 0–87691–214–5

Library of Congress Cataloging in Publication Data
Main entry under title:

The American fisherman's fresh and salt water guide.

    Bibliography: p.
    Includes index.
    SUMMARY: Experts discuss their fishing specialties such as Eastern trout, panfish, Atlantic salmon, and big bass.

    1. Fishing.   2. Fishing—United States.
    [1. Fishing]   I. Sparano, Vin T.
SH441.A46   799.1′2′0937   75–37572
ISBN 0–87691–214–5

Published by Winchester Press
205 East 42nd Street, New York 10017

Printed in the United States of America

Contents

Foreword

VIN T. SPARANO

If I had my choice of any fishing partner for a certain species of fish, whom would I pick? That's the question I asked myself when I first began to outline this book, and it's the question that led me to the top fishing experts in the country today. It would be great, I thought, to catch salmon with the legendary Lee Wulff, to cast for bonefish with superb fly-rod man Lefty Kreh, to fish the famed Catskill streams with *Outdoor Life*'s Fishing Editor Jerry Gibbs, and so on.

The first step was to take a map of the United States and label it by species. Over New England I marked "Eastern Trout"; the Florida area I labeled "Fishing the Flats"; the Rocky Mountain States, "Western Trout"; Washington and Oregon, "The Steelhead"; and so on. I stopped marking the map when I felt I had the 12 most popular fish and fishing in the United States. The complete list makes up the contents page of this book.

After I had picked the species and areas, I went after the experts . . . the guys who know what it's all about. As Senior Editor of *Outdoor Life,* I already knew most of these men and I had fished with more than half of them. I called Lefty Kreh, who many years ago showed me how to drive a Honey Blonde streamer into a 15-knot wind on Barnegat Bay for striped bass. I know of no man today who can match Lefty's skill with a fly rod on the flats, and I was happy when he agreed to write a chapter on this specialized fishing.

I spoke to Jerry Gibbs, who has shared with me the agony of getting skunked on New Jersey Reservoirs and the ecstasy of unbelievable fishing in the waters off Montauk, New York. I've seen Jerry whip very big fish with very tiny rods, but he's at his best when conning the incomparable Eastern trout . . . one of the spookiest fish in the world. Jerry said O.K. and wrote the chapter on Eastern trout.

A trip down the hall of the *Outdoor Life* offices was all it took to persuade Bill Vogt, the magazine's Conservation Editor, to reminisce about his youth in the Midwest where panfish and catfish are accorded the reputations they deserve. Bill crammed a lifetime of panfish know-how into his chapter.

Then up to New England to coax noted sportsman Lee Wulff to write about his first angling love, the Atlantic salmon. Next to Wyoming to ask Charles Waterman, a pro on Western trout fishing, to tell us about the famous fish of the Madison, the Yellowstone, and the many other Western trout waters.

At times I felt like the sheriff in an old movie rounding up a posse of the fastest guns in the West . . . except I was looking for the best fishermen in North America. The line-up was starting to look better and better.

Bruce Brady, for example, whose stomping grounds are the bass waters of the South, tells readers all they need to know about catching big bass. Bruce, incidentally, is Midsouth Field Editor for *Outdoor Life*. Bob Cary, a long-time outdoor writer and sportsman who now feeds his soul with the woods and waters of Minnesota, writes about his small war with the muskellunge.

Milt Rosko and Mark Sosin, both good friends of mine, were chosen for their extraordinary knowledge in certain areas. Milt, who can pull striped bass off a slippery jetty at 3 A.M., when and where no one else can, is an expert on inshore fishing. Mark is an accomplished offshore big-game fisherman who knows what, when, and how to fish for the big blue-water fish.

John Cartier, *Outdoor Life*'s Midwest Field Editor and a man who knows all there is to know about Lake Michigan coho, came through with an inside look at the fantastic coho miracle. Farther West, I asked Larry Green, another pro-angler, to tell about fishing the inshore waters of the Pacific. Emmit Glanz, well-known steelhead expert, was the logical choice for that species.

I had my posse . . . a team of the very best fishermen . . . and within a year the entire book was in manuscript form and in the hands of Winchester Press.

What did these experts write about? I gave them little, if any, direction. I simply said, "Tell the reader all the important things he should know about your favorite fish or fishing." What I got was a wealth of information on popular fresh and saltwater fishing from Florida to Oregon. I learned when to fish for certain species and where to look for them. I found loads of solid information on tackle, lures, techniques. The data and advice is also aimed at a wide audience . . . from the purist after Atlantic salmon in Labrador to the catfisherman in Missouri.

Winchester Press asked me to contribute three chapters and I decided to stick close to basic how-to subjects. I enjoy fishing with natural and live baits and sometimes catching the bait is as much fun as the fishing. Learning how and when to catch the various baits adds a new dimension to fishing, and my chapter on natural baits shows how.

Another chapter, "Don't Spoil Your Fish," covers a favorite subject of mine . . . field care and cleaning of fish. I've seen too many fish wasted on docks, banks, and boats across the country. If you've killed a fish, take it home and eat it. Learn to respect your quarry. My last chapter is on knots, a subject for both novice and experienced angler.

So here it is . . . the best of the experts. Whether you are a novice or an experienced fisherman, there is something here for you. Just pick the fish or the type of fishing you're interested in and you can be sure that the advice you're getting is from a guy who knows his apples.

Good Luck and Good Fishing.

Lee Wulff

An early morning start for the salmon waters of the Serpentine River in Newfoundland.

The Atlantic Salmon

LEE WULFF

Concerning the Atlantic salmon we, in the United States, are not at the crossroads. We have already taken the wrong road and are now slowly trying to work our way back. We are making a belated but dedicated effort to bring back this great gamefish to the New England rivers where it was once so plentiful that few believed the stocks could ever be exhausted. But we let them disappear from all but a few small rivers in Maine by ladderless dams, pollution, and the ruin of their habitat. Now state, federal, and private funds and energies are united in a drive to restore the salmon to their native streams.

It is interesting to note that back in the 1870's an effort was mounted to restore the Atlantic salmon to the Connecticut River. The project was successful enough to bring back a few hundred salmon for a good start but they were caught almost exclusively by the commercial netters at the rivermouth. Since the state of Connecticut, at that time, would not forbid commercial fishing, the sportsmen who had spearheaded the drive lost interest and the commercial fishermen wouldn't spend their own money or interest in the necessary support of the venture.

Now our federal and state governments are spending millions on hatcheries and research for the restoration. The International Atlantic Salmon Foundation, a public-spirited group of anglers, has raised $1.5

million to construct a research center near the United States–Canadian border which will work under Canadian management to develop the genetic strains required both for the United States restoration and for maximum returns in the Canadian rivers.

Restoration of Atlantic Salmon in America, Inc. is aiding with funds and information, and promotes public support for the salmon restoration. They point out the need for fishways where they were overlooked long ago and for the water quality and good river management necessary to do the job. The salmon should soon be coming back to New England.

In the rest of the North Atlantic salmon areas in Canada and Europe, the salmon stocks have been diminished but there is still angling for thousands in what may be a dwindling opportunity. In the early 1960's commercial netters found the feeding ground of the north Atlantic salmon. In spite of a heavy take by the development of this new high-seas fishery, salmon are still being taken by angling on the Canadian salmon streams and, in the province of Newfoundland, where more than half the Canadian commercial catch has always been taken, commercial netting is still going on.

But the management battle there is far from won. The management on the rivers open to the public has resulted in constant diminution of the runs and of the size of fish that make up the runs. An example of the lack of wisdom of Canadian management is that for over 40 years there has been a federal law in effect that insists on a minimum mesh size for commercial nets. This size net permits the grilse or "dwarf" salmon to pass through the nets and go on to the spawning grounds while the superior, larger, more salable salmon are caught by their gills in the meshes. As a result, rivers which had a run of big salmon now have runs made up of the same numbers (or an even smaller number) of dwarf, one-year-sea-feeding fish.

Any cattle breeder, any grower of vegetables, selects his best stock for seed. He doesn't sell his prize bulls for hamburger. He tries to build up the size and strength of his stock. And, in the case of Atlantic salmon, the preferred big fish which, by heredity, stay at sea to feed for two or three years before they return to their rivers for their first spawning, will have eaten less, rather than more, of the limited stream food supply available in their nursery streams. The same stream food supply that now brings back fish averaging 4 pounds could well bring back instead, as it once did, an equal number of fish four times as heavy.

Lee Wulff hangs on to a battling Atlantic salmon on a river in Labrador.

It is hard to understand why the Canadian biologists have let this ridiculous system of harvest go on for generations without protest. It still goes on and, until the Canadian management changes its viewpoint, the salmon fishing in the Atlantic provinces will decline.

The time to go Atlantic salmon fishing in Canada and the rest of the world is now, before the fishing becomes even more expensive and harder to find. Fishing is still within the budget of the average angler if he can spare the necessary time or wants to take a few years' savings for the trip or both.

A group traveling together in a car can drive to Nova Scotia or Newfoundland and Labrador where all the rivers are open to any licensed angler. (License fees increased sharply for nonresidents in 1975, in recognition of the scarcity and angling value of this particular fish.) An angler may camp out or stay at a nearby motel or fishing camp. And he'll need a guide or half-a-guide, since one guide may serve two nonresidents instead of one if they prefer it.

There is some open water on the Miramichi and other streams in New Brunswick and some "public" water and public streams in Quebec, like the Matane River on the south shore near the mouth of the St.

3

Lawrence River. Local accomodations are reasonable. Again, guides are required for nonresidents and one guide may serve two anglers.

From these relatively humble costs, salmon fishing rises in expense to where it costs $2,000 per week per angler on the Jupiter River on Anticosti Island in Quebec. And, on many waters leased or owned by individuals or clubs, there is just no way any angler, no matter how rich, can hope to join in the fishing without an invitation.

Before condemning the high prices and restrictions, it is well to consider that the owners or lessee pay for the salmon fishing and pay for adequate protection and that, without their payments and protection, that superb salmon fishing they get would not even exist. It is wise to recognize that *nowhere, ever,* has public management of Atlantic salmon fishing prevented the fishing from deteriorating or disappearing altogether. The "average" fisherman and the average fishing manager don't realize how much protection they need. There are not enough salmon to go around, and to try to spread them around to all those who want to fish for them is certain to bring disaster for the salmon.

So, fish for Atlantic salmon and enjoy the unique problem of trying to reach a great gamefish's mind, or his memory, instead of his stomach. For the salmon, on his return to fresh water, is not a feeder but a well-fed fish with a great store of energy. He has entered a fasting period he won't really break until he's headed back to the sea again, if and when he survives the spawning period. And, knowing that these fish are unusual and special and their future is uncertain, be glad that the angling opportunity is yours. Study them. Cast well. Fish long and hard and, over the years, it is almost certain that you'll come to love them, as I do.

Since they have no hunger, don't look for salmon in the spots where you'd look for trout, even though you may be using trout tackle and trout flies. Seek them where the slow currents will flow soothingly over their restless bodies. They lie where the water is deep enough for their safety with a good pool or deep run close by to speed to in case of danger. Knowing he can get away swiftly to that open run or pool, a salmon may let you approach quite close to him but, if he's seen you, the chances are your flies won't tempt him unless you're willing to freeze into a position for 30 minutes or more until he comes to think of you as a tree stump or a strange-shaped rock that suddenly settled where none was before and proceeds to ignore you.

Lee Wulff casts to a good salmon lie.

Joan Wulff tails a salmon.

In high water the salmon tend to hang in the current where it slows down enough to give them comfort without having to swim too hard to hold their positions. As the water drops and the current slows, they tend to move farther toward the head of the pool (where the current is about the same as that they settled in at high water) and back to the tail of the pool where the water quickens before pouring out.

To cover all the water is to spend a lot of time where there are no salmon to catch. The good salmon fisherman can spot where the salmon lies or has learned where they lie through experience. In very clear streams it is easy to see the salmon and to fish only for the salmon one sees. When the water is peat-stained to a cloudy brown and the fish are invisible, it takes a knowing angler to concentrate his fishing where the salmon are. The fishermen who are able to do this will catch a lot of fish while the angler who knows neither salmon fishing nor that particular stretch of the river well will go without a rise, wasting his casts in empty water. A wise angler, reaching a pool before other anglers do, can cover in a matter of minutes those special spots where salmon rest and take flies best. The odds are that another angler coming along to fish the pool soon afterward will have nowhere near the chance the first fisherman had.

The conventional and most productive method of fishing for salmon is with a wet fly at the usual cross-stream angle of 45 degrees down and across the current. The cast should straighten out and the fly should start to move as soon as the current catches it. Normally it will swim just below the surface and a salmon in taking it will usually show himself. The classic rise to a wet fly is the "head and tail" in which the fish's head breaks the surface as his mouth opens to take the fly and he rolls on up and shows his back and dorsal fin and then his tail as he heads down again. If the fly is "hitched" to make it skim the surface (two half-hitches are tied just behind the head of the fly) the taking salmon will usually show his head well but will not come as far out of the water and will not, in most cases, show the dorsal and tail as well.

The Portland Creek hitch, or riffling hitch, which came to the world through my fishing camps there, makes a fly skim the surface or "riffle." This puts a wet fly halfway to becoming a dry fly. It brings the salmon to the surface for the rise and is more fun to fish than a wet fly. It will bring to the fly many a fish that has ignored a conventional wet fly and is a way of fishing every salmon angler should understand. The fly skitters only when under tension. To fish the hitch well, the angler's casts should straighten out perfectly. The single-hooked fly must ride with the bend facing downstream. This is accomplished by putting the half-hitches on the same side of the fly that the current moves to, as you face it.

Salmon are a moody fish. At times they'll rise to take a fly the first time it passes within striking range. More often they'll move up slightly toward it as it passes and then return to their safe and comfortable lie. If it comes again they may rise and take it or rise and miss it. They may miss it deliberately or they may miss it unintentionally. If an angler watches his wet fly constantly he'll see the faint flash of the fish as it makes even the slightest move toward his fly . . . or the boil that may

*Atlantic salmon fighting
and conquering the falls
on the Humber River,
Newfoundland.*

A vanquished salmon on an Icelandic River.

result from a more determined near-miss. To be looking away at that moment and to continue to move on down through the pool is to miss a great chance to hook a salmon.

Once an angler locates such a "taking" fish, he should stop in his tracks, judge the exact amount of line he has out at the time, and continue to cast for a few times to that salmon's location. If he fails to elicit a rise in a few casts, it's wise to rest the fish and wait for a few minutes before casting again either with the same fly or a different fly. Changing flies will often tempt reluctant fish to take. I like to change the character of the fly rather than the pattern; shape and size rather than color, and I rarely leave a fish I haven't been able to hook without giving him one last chance at the fly that first drew his attention.

Because of a salmon's considerable size and its monetary value ($25 or more for a 10-pound fish), protecting the salmon is paramount. It is for this reason that conventional salmon flies, unweighted, are required by law. Trebles are barred, save in very small sizes in Quebec. In Europe, where a smaller, controlled number of anglers are permitted to fish the private waters, trebles and weights are allowed because the number of fish taken from each "beat" or river can be controlled. The owner or lessee knows the anglers and their character. A poor sport can be barred from the water. In public waters nothing is controlled but the limit (by possession) and the method (surface fly only), which holds down foul hooking. Were trebles and weighted flies allowed, the salmon on the public waters would have disappeared long ago. The fish are too big and too vulnerable to stand against snagging.

Poaching has become a paramount problem on many Canadian rivers. Unfortunately, there is a strong feeling that it is morally "right" for a poor Canadian to steal salmon by poaching from the rich Canadians and Americans who own or lease the waters they want to fish. It is not a matter of morals. It is simply a matter of letting enough salmon spawn to preserve the runs. There are not enough salmon to go around. Someone must do without. Those who cannot afford it do not realize that without the private water and the protection owners and lessee pay for, the salmon on most rivers would be long gone.

A wet fly covers a great deal of water. As an angler works down through a pool his fly traces path after path, each a short distance from and parallel to the one that preceded it. Every salmon in a well-fished pool will see the angler's fly. But when it comes to dry flies, which travel much more slowly and travel directly with the current instead of angling across it, the fly covers only a small part of the pool. Since it gives a lesser coverage the angler must be able to concentrate his fishing with the dry fly where the fish are concentrated in order to maintain an equal chance to bring a fish to his hook. Therefore the dry fly is more effective in low water when the fish are more concentrated than when, in high water, they are more widely spread out through the streams.

The dry fly is fished most effectively with a completely free float just as if fishing for a wise old brown trout. The strike should be slow and deliberate. After a while an accomplished dry fly angler will learn to watch the fly and never strike unless he sees the fish actually take it. Salmon will rise to a dry fly and bunt it with their noses. I've seen them poke their chins up and push a dry fly under to drown it without ever opening their mouths. If a new salmon angler sees rises like this he will think the fish has taken the fly and he'll strike and fail to hook. Then he'll strike slower, then faster, and yet, unless the fish actually takes the fly into its mouth, he'll miss each rise . . . and he'll be mighty confused!

Wet flies have a long and great tradition behind them. The Scots developed their tying to an art. Knowing the work and skill that went into the tying of a perfect Jock Scott or Mar Lodge, an angler somehow feels a salmon should appreciate it and therefore rise to it. The time-tested patterns have a great record of effectiveness as well as beauty. I wouldn't be on the river without a few . . . but I know that carelessly thrown together bits of feather and fur will often work as well or better and that unusual sizes and shapes often take the difficult fish.

The whole dry fly spectrum is relatively new, developed within the last 50 years. This has given many of us a great chance to develop new and effective patterns. There are still hundreds of color schemes that have yet to be tried in dry flies and hundreds of variations in shape to try. And each successful one will have a story behind it.

One of my secret weapons, the surface stonefly, a dry that lies in the surface film and barely floats, is an oversize imitation of the stoneflies to be found in practically every salmon river. It is difficult to fish. Its flotation is so low that if it drops to the water from a foot above the surface it will sink. To be sure it will float I have to skid it onto the surface as I'd land a seaplane. Once on the water it's hard to see (for the angler, that is, not the fish). It takes trouble to fish it but when I

Lee Wulff works a salmon in close.

Lee Wulff readies a tired salmon for the hand grip.

do, I know that although the salmon I fish for may have seen 100 artificial flies in the last few days, he hasn't seen this one . . . and that it may be just the one he's been dreaming about ever since he left the river as a smolt, for his long ocean voyage.

Another wet fly, named for my wife, the Lady Joan, is quite conventional but uses a mixture of squirrel tail and black-bear hair for the wing and has a burnt-orange body with a wrap of gold tinsel behind a bright yellow throat. It's a slim, low-water fly, and it skims well because of the bear hair in the wing. I wanted a dark fly because black is the most conspicuous color when viewed by a fish upward against the light and I wanted a strong but unusual color to complement it. It is basically orange and black with a touch of white and yellow. It has worked well, particularly when "hitched."

Salmon are difficult to bring to a fly but not as stereotyped in their rising as a wise old brown trout. They will take a dragging dry fly. They'll often come to a skittered skater or bivisible with a savage rush. They can be tempted, sometimes, by twitching a dry fly just as it passes over their noses . . . even by sinking it at that point and letting it continue on in a wet state. I usually save such tactics until I am ready to give up on a fish. I believe, generally, that the traditional methods will work best, year in and year out.

Similarly, with wet flies, one may vary the usual swing by letting them drift freely, just under the surface. And then, hopefully, just ahead of a salmon lie, have the fly start moving and make its conventional swing across the current.

When it comes to playing a salmon one can have a magnificent challenge. By using standard trout tackle and adding 100 yards or more of backing, a fisherman can get a tackle problem impossible to find on a trout stream. After playing salmon on trout tackle the playing of trout loses much of its luster. Having caught a 27-pound Atlantic salmon with a No. 16 single-hook dry fly on a 6-foot 1.6-ounce rod, I find it hard to find a similar tackle challenge with any trout.

A stream that has a magnificent run one year at a given time and a pool that produces well one year may offer poor fishing the next. Salmon enter the streams at the whim of the water temperatures and may be as much as three weeks later one year than they were the preceding one. To go salmon fishing and give up because of one bad experience is to fail to understand it and give the fishing a chance.

A rare feat—Lee Wulff with a 30-pound Atlantic salmon taken on a 2½-ounce 7-foot fly rod. The trophy fish was landed on the Serpentine River, Newfoundland.

A brace of fresh-run Atlantic salmon.

The luckiest salmon fishermen are those who can fish for at least a week at a time and who fish year after year in order to average out. An angler on expensive private waters may have a bad week while an angler on a public stream may have exceptional fishing. They are a paradoxical fish that no one will understand completely, but if we lose them, angling will be much, much poorer for their loss. If you haven't fished for Atlantic salmon there's not likely, for a long time, to be a better time to start than now.

*Well-loved section below
Five-Arch Bridge on New
York's Esopus Creek, usually
produces trout for anglers
willing to work hard.*

*Local anglers on Esopus
Creek have developed long
rod technique for dapping
minnows into pockets—a
killer on both browns and
rainbows.*

14

The Way
of the Eastern Trout

JERRY GIBBS

Down below the five-arch bridge on New York's Esopus Creek there's a boulder we call Rock-of-the-Broken-Shin, for good reason. There, a good fishing companion did a near green splint on his left leg following me to a good spot where we did not catch fish. Walking and thinking about the episode again, I tromped into the morning solitude of an angler whose face told of the sort of rapture known only to fishermen and lovers.

I did not want to bother him but he waved me over where we talked without exchanging names the way you certainly have done. It was spring and the sun came out, sparking the little white flecks of spray where the current broke over river rocks. My friend stood to the top of his boots, streaming line-with-nymph downriver where no fish was interested.

"I could take 100 years of this," he said.

"With a few more trout thrown in," I added, as I started to leave.

"Oh, there'll be some. You just have to keep coming back."

And now 100 years have passed, or so it seems to me, in fishing places near and far, but most of all in change. The years-sacred doctrines of our foremost angling authorities are no longer inviolate—even on the remaining Eastern waters where they were written. Cyclic and man-made changes have altered insect life. Time, travel, and the desire to become reasonably proficient in other areas of angling, more and more draw us from the reproduction of exacting fly patterns. The changes in fly-tying art, for not too dissimilar reasons, roughly parallel the development of art on canvas, though much more slowly. There are limitations to our acceptances by salmonoid critics, however—which is probably not a limitation on their part at all—and so within the impressionistic fly tying school it is now materials that are undergoing the greatest experimentation.

The very courses and flows of rivers have also changed. Some rivers have given way to expansive lakes where rainbows and browns must be taken in over 100-foot depths by trolling strange clanking devices seemingly better suited to stave off crows.

Still, we keep coming back. Why, if there are oceans of giants, or broad-shouldered rivers in Montana and Wyoming where backcasts never snarl? Part of the answer is the sense of history, for it was on the waters of the Northeastern states that serious American trout fishing commenced.

Part of the answer must also be a fevered state of mind, not uncommon among fishermen, for how, rationally, after whipping a giant tarpon on a flyrod, can you find excitement in catching a trout that may stretch a mere 10 or 13 inches in length? Credit must be taken by the fish himself, for that size-13-or-under trout can provide exasperation, frustration, and finally humiliation far beyond his size. He is a splendid mixture of intellectual and primeval challenge to our most sophisticated way of life. Having been scorned for a day or more by the resident trout population in some pastoral Eastern stream is enough to send an iron-nerved executive into a fit of depthless depression.

We begin to doubt our abilities to ever catch any fish anywhere, and we hate especially these cosmopolitan trout while secretly loving them. For if we keep returning, we shall be rewarded with magical days that exceed even our most outrageous angling fantasies; days when we will coax and hook the most stubbornly closed-mouth trout from impossible-to-reach places during balmy cloudless days at the wrong time of year. And we will go home exuberant, buoyant, as light-hearted as children. I once found the most sour-dispositioned angler I know walking down a dirt trail one summer's dusk, and he was singing aloud.

16

The Way of the Eastern Trout

Eastern trout fishing at its finest, to my way of choosing, is an intimate kind of fishing. This is a state of mind, to be sure, for there are some burly brawling rivers in this part of the country, and others with deep secret currents quite powerful enough to whisk your feet from under you. But the country, often as not, comes up close to the river banks to greet you in the East, and even if there are mountains somewhere close behind, the trees and wrinkles in the land mostly hide them from your view. My overall impression of Western fishing, by comparison, is one of far vistas, rolling foothills and snowcapped peaks showing purple and blue in the distance.

There are three kinds of good trout fishing in the Northeast: The remaining stretches of the famous rivers when they are uncrowded; little

Small streams like this that run into larger, better known rivers, often hold many of the good rainbows and browns northeastern anglers think have been caught after the first month or two of the trout season. The trout seek cooler, well-oxygenated water of the brooks. Later in the season they often choose the small streams in which to spawn.

Bill Rooney nets a nice brown trout from NJ's Round Valley reservoir. Lake is noted for large rainbows.

brooks and streams that you must find yourself by brush busting or through the grace of friends; and lakes and ponds which hold large trout that are getting bigger every year. You will find all three classifications of trout waters from Maine to Virginia, some areas having more of one kind than the others, naturally.

It's splendid adventure journeying to new waters, of course, but there is really no need to. I remember an afternoon's talk with fly tyers Harry and Else Darbee whose names are bywords among fly fishermen throughout the country. We traveled verbally to far away exotic rivers talking of the salmon and trout we had caught. Before we went to look at his roosters, Harry ended the conversation on this note.

"It's all wonderful," he said, "but I've got more than enough to keep me busy right here."

The Darbees' home streams are New York's Beaverkill and Willowemoc, famous for years, often unjustly cursed as fished-out, and still providing strong lure to anglers from many places in the land.

The point is, if it's the fishing itself to which you're addicted, there is so much to learn about the changing moods of just one stretch of river,

18

that you can very easily devote most of an angling lifetime to a single area. When, after years of studying and fishing it, you have come to know the trout, the hatches of each season, the methods that will consistently make you more successful than others who fish your stream casually, familiarity of your river will continue to please you each time you return to it. This attitude, too, is part of Eastern trout angling.

There are a handful of rivers among the famous on which I think you will have some interesting times if you ever fish them. They are not necessarily the best or the most acclaimed, but they are good because they can be maddening, glorious, perverse, and fun—all within very short periods of time.

I like Vermont's Lamoille because it holds up well all summer long. There are sections of slowly rolling deep currents, and near the town of Morrisville, a long underwater ridge splits the stream for quite a stretch. You can walk along the ridge with chest-high waders, and fish to the far bank where browns and rainbows will roll for creamy fur-emerging-pattern nymphs on summer evenings.

There are big fish in the river here, many of them, and if you fish it long enough, some time when trout are being foolish and eating your flies with uncommon frequency, you will be utterly shocked when one of the fish you pull in turns out to be a yellow perch!

Almost everyone who stops at the famous Orvis shop in Manchester, Vermont, to examine bamboo rods and ogle the beastly size trout they keep in their pools, will eventually try fishing the Battenkill. This river gets a lot of pressure during spring and tourist season, and the trout consequently become rather put off by the usual flies and other lures they see so often.

Many anglers feel the Battenkill no longer holds the number of fish or quality of fish it did only recent years ago, but this is not true. I have seen what just one shocking test produced from a short stretch of the river. The fish are there, big browns mostly, and brook trout in the feeders.

At normal suppertime, when most anglers have quit, I've often waded across the river near East Arlington to fish a pool where children and dogs, a short while before, had been turning the water to froth. Everyone fishes from the near bank here, and I think my different angle of presentation is what causes the trout to respond so well. Or maybe it's suppertime for them, too.

Erik Lyngse fishes a small Vermont creek for brook trout. Many small streams like this scattered throughout the Northeast offer surprisingly good fishing for native brookies, rainbows and brown trout.

I know where an owl lives on the lower Battenkill, a great horned owl, I think, by the deep requiem voice he has. When he wakes me at night I cannot get back to sleep for a long time and so walk down to the river. If an owl like that gives you chills, the sounds on the water will double them. What kind of trout makes explosive splashes like that? If you do not mind night fishing, persistence here will eventually show you these night river noises are created by truly huge browns.

Everyone says only the smallest flies work during daylight hours on the Battenkill, but sometime, when all else fails, try dapping long hackle spiders on a breeze and see what happens.

I've had wonderful days on most of the well-known Catskill rivers, but it is Esopus Creek to which I keep returning. The reason is, I'm sure, the water's manic nature. For extreme moodiness the Esopus is hard to equal. This river has a built-in excuse-for-fishlessness, too. It is

Jerry Gibbs returns from an evening's fishing on Vermont's Lamoille River with a nice brown trout taken on a Hendrickson nymph in midsummer. Same nymph took many more rainbows and browns for him the same evening while many duns were on the water.

Fly-caught native brook trout from small streams throughout the Northeast.

the portal at the village of Shandaken, releasing via 18 miles of under-mountain passage a flow from the Schoharie River to the north. An open portal can be neatly blamed for turning the Esopus overly cold, too high, and silty. When it is closed for too long you can complain over a lack of water, extreme clarity, or rising water temperatures. It's really wonderful. The Esopus has a good early season rainbow run some years, and there are browns in the river, too.

Local anglers have developed an extremely effective technique using long rods and live or preserved minnows which are dropped into likely holes and pools. You can use all the other angling methods, too, on the Esopus, but the river provides some excellent fly fishing if it chooses.

There are long glides, deep pools and riffly rock-studded stretches from which to choose. The main difficulty, as with so many of New York's readily accessible, well-known waters, is the fishing pressure. If you work at it, however, you will be able to locate spots that allow you some solitude.

Though called a creek, the Esopus has some swift powerful stretches and very strong currents that can fool you, as my good friend and fishing companion Dave Kemp once experienced north of Phoenicia. We were working a midstream run with deeply sunken streamers, wading in that tip-toe fashion that you use when you are too deep for safety. David suddenly disappeared from sight. His return to light was done with great majesty and the only thing to indicate that the episode was not altogether a casual performance that occurred with some frequency was the splintered tip of his beautiful new Fenwick fly rod.

My suggestion for taking fish from this river is to switch water types frequently when one type is not producing. If that doesn't work, try fishing up into the many feeders that supply the main river.

Freestone rivers, like those I have mentioned so far, require some mileage to support trout. By comparison, the classic limestone streams found in Pennsylvania do not. These extremely fertile streams have a great trout-carrying capacity. Food from just one short stretch of water will support a large number of fish. As the doyen of the Letort once said to me, "All you really need to fish these waters is not a lot of elbow room, but quiet." Charles Fox knows whereof he speaks. Along with master angler Vince Marinaro, Fox is responsible for developing the sophisticated methods that take monstrous brown trout from these tiny streams.

22

Joe Peters fishes a slow section of the East Branch of New York's Delaware River. Many sections of some Catskill rivers see few anglers despite being near major population centers.

Joe Peters and his son Mark try some spin casting on East Branch of Delaware in New York state. River offers potential for good float fishing as well as wading and bank fishing.

A Pennsylvanian fishes the hard root networks on the Yellow Breeches. Many Eastern streams require extremely short casts to such difficult places.

Ultrafine tackle is needed on waters like the Yellow Breeches, and especially Big Spring, Falling Spring, and the Letort, where some sections are reserved for fly fishing or fish-for-fun (no kill) only. The ubiquitous Muddler Minnow can be successful on these streams, but you should have them in a variety of sizes. Extremely selective, trout in the limestones may choose to feed on crayfish of a particular size, scorning anything larger or smaller.

Scoop a handful of watercress from the near bank of one of these streams and you will soon see the food available to the trout here. Besides the numerous cress or sow bugs, you will find ample quantities of fresh water shrimp. Flys that imitate these crustaceans—worked on 6X tippets with sharp jigging actions away from the fish—are extremely successful in spring and late season. Cress bug imitations, dead-drifted or slowly drawn away from a fish, are also excellent at these times.

The Jassids in colors from green (early in the season) to dark (later on), ants, and other terrestrials in Size 22 or smaller, are now standard

Willard Johns of the Pennsylvania Fish Commission fishes watercress-choked Big Spring Creek. Pennsylvania's famous limestones support extremely large browns for such small waters.

on the limestones. Different streams have different major hatches like the blue-winged and pale sulphers, the little dark and light olives, and the flies of the Caenidae family whose imitations are best fished on 6 to 7X tippets. Before you fish for the fiendishly fussy trout in these waters, drop into Ed Koch's tackle shop in Boiling Spring to make sure you have the flies for the current hatch.

Great beds of watercress and elodea frequently make fly presentation extremely difficult on the limestones—especially since the small size of the waters usually precludes wading. You will work yourself weary trying for a particular trout—the angling here is very definitely of the sight type where you cast to individual fish—and then when you have given up and are moving on, the sullen brown that may be several or more pounds will splash outrageously taking an invisible morsel from the surface film, and leave you shattered. There are 5-, 8-, and 10-pounders possible from these streams—enough lure to bring you back again and again despite what it does to your nervous system.

Many lakes close to large popula-
tion centers are now providing
much of the trout sport in the
Northeast that was once provided
by rivers. Management programs,
including regular stocking, keep
rainbow and brown populations
at a high level from spring
through winter. Trout grow faster
in empoundments, too. Here Jerry
Gibbs holds a stringer of early
season trout from a northern New
Jersey lake.

Oil company road maps used in conjunction with county maps are your ticket for discovering the many tiny brooks that exist throughout states in the East. Many times you will, I'm sure, find yourself heading for these tiny waters in preference to the larger lakes and rivers. The main reason is solitude—especially on weekends. Many of the smaller brooks in the Northeast run through private property. You will usually be all right, however, if you make your stream entry from a road or with permission of a landowner. Following a stream can take you through private property for which permission to trespass may not have been gained, but only occasionally will you run into complaining landowners.

Pet dogs can present a threat. Dr. Mark Canter, a fishing companion

26

of mine, exhibited lightninglike thinking and extreme sacrifice some years ago when approached by a team composed of one large, roaring German shepherd and an equally ferocious Doberman. Mark was in the stream and the snarling beasts were also preparing to enter it, with obvious intent.

"I had two good rainbows," the good doctor will tell you, "and there was only one thing to do. I threw one of the fish to them. They went away immediately. And so did I."

Many small lakes or ponds offer excellent trout fishing throughout the Northeast. To my taste, the most delightful angling between the extremes of large reservoirs and rivers is the trouting on Cape Cod's small freshwater ponds. Here you can take rainbows, browns, and sometimes brook trout. Brown trout have been taken weighing in the high 'teens. Nestled among the pines, these little lakes provide good sport year-round, though in the summer you must fish around 40 feet in the thermocline. The natural forage in reclaimed ponds is crayfish. Once overrun by rough fish, the reclaimed waters were poisoned and then restocked. Now natural bait minnows are forbidden. The trout grow well on a crustacean diet, their flesh bright red-orange and fat.

In some ponds, anglers use grass shrimp taken from beneath the sod banks of Cape Cod Bay and kept in sawdust or seaweed. The trout do not seem to mind that these little shrimp have come from salt water at all. You can use flyrods and streamers on these ponds, with a lead core shooting head or fast sinking line needed for the warm weather. Spinners and spoons cast far out and allowed to sink are also very good baits. Early in the season many anglers troll with flies.

One thing to remember if you try these ponds is that even in summer, when most of the fishing is deep, early and late in the day the fish will leave the depths and cruise fairly close to the shore in search of food—especially crayfish, which they can scoop up easily in the shallows.

I have fond memories of canoe fishing the little Cape ponds such as Baker, Mashpee-Wakeby, Shubael and Hamblin. Angling for trout is a somewhat different experience here, for the smell of salt is continually in the air and a short drive in any direction will bring you to the Atlantic or large salt-water bays.

Many larger lakes throughout the Northeast hold rainbows and brown trout of truly colossal proportions. Maine, New Hampshire, Vermont, Massachusetts, New York, Pennsylvania, and even New Jersey

27

have such lakes. Fish and game departments are continually evaluating management programs that result in fisheries for these big trout.

The best way for you, as an angler, to determine the status of a given lake, including your chances of taking good trout there, is to contact your local fish commission's public information department. You can obtain up-to-date catch figures, the best months and the tackle used.

ROD & REEL RECOMMENDATIONS FOR EASTERN TROUT

Rods

Type	Material	Length	Action
Fly	Bamboo, Fiberglass, Graphite	6 to 8½ feet	Fast and slow.
Spinning	Fiberglass	5½ to 7 feet	Slow to medium.
Casting	Fiberglass or Graphite	5½ to 6 feet	Stiff bass action with straight handle. For trolling only.
Live Bait	Cane or Fiberglass	10 to 12 feet	Slow. Special purpose rod for dapping baits in pockets of rivers.

Reels

Type	Specifications
Fly	Single action preferable for most situations. Multiplying retrieve may be desirable in lake situations and on the largest, fastest rivers.
Spinning	Smooth, nonskipping drag is vitally important—especially when line tests of 4- and 7-pound are used. Capacity of 180 yards of 4-pound is usually sufficient.
Bait Casting (revolving spool)	Oversize double handles (as used by bass anglers). Smooth star drag vital. Good fit of side plates to spool flange so line will not slip around spool axis. For trolling only.

28

I have done well in Pepacton Reservoir in New York's Catskills on brown trout, at times, in Round Valley in New Jersey on rainbows, and in the same state's Spruce Run Reservoir which houses large browns.

The most productive methods for catching trout in lakes is trolling or drifting live minnows. This is not my favorite kind of fishing—especially in New York water supply reservoirs where you must row to troll—but if it's large fish you're after, then you ought to investigate this type of angling whatever the state.

Early and late in the year, live drifted bait is more successful, though it can still take huge fish right through summer. During the hot weather, in lakes that develop a definite thermocline, trolling has to be the outstanding producer. The trolling involved is not the sort that begins and ends with throwing out some casting lure and merely streaming it behind your boat.

Deep trolling is what is indicated here, using everything from diving planers like the Pink Lady, to downriggers with 7- to 12-pound weights. Now that reasonably priced, portable downriggers are available you'll see more and more small boats equipped with the devices which permit accurate controlled lure presentation at precise depths—extremely important when trout are holding in a preferred temperature zone.

Along with equipment that helps you get your lures to the fish, you'll find the multi-spinner attractors that simulate baitfish schools are very effective in bringing strikes when trout ignore single lure offerings. Where the thermocline (or preferred temperature comfort zone) rests on or close to a bar, point of land, underwater island that is surrounded by deeper water, you'll find a natural fish magnet around which to work your lake troll or drift your bait. Bluffs around shore with the same characteristics are worthwhile to try.

Eastern anglers, like fishermen everywhere, are too often concerned entirely with matching seasonal hatches, while ignoring the progression of daily cycle times. The early season result typically finds you bellied up to the local watering hole after unsuccessfully beating a stream to death all morning. If you had long-range eyesight, it might shock you to see the river that you just left suddenly begin yielding a superhatch of Quill Gordons just when you were certain the season was yet too young. Daily emergence times vary as the season progresses, which should clue you to vary your efforts.

Early in the season waters begin to warm later in the day, and any

Erik Lyngse casts for big browns on section of Vermont's Winooski River. This river, like many in East, is subjected to great fluctations throughout the year due to draw-downs, flow controls.

hatch that's going to occur will usually do so in the afternoon. As the season ages, the hatches occur later and later, finally into dusk, then dark. As this happens, however, the morning hatches are beginning. In the warmer weather, then, dawn and evening are your best hatch periods. In summer, the dusk hours are not enough to cool the water, and the evening hatches begin to taper off. Your better hatch period is early morning in mid- to late July. In autumn, the hatch period begins moving back toward midday and finally afternoon, just where it was at the season's start.

Yes, there are hatches after July. The Caenidae family's Tricorythodes will hatch into September or later, and the Baetis, the olives—specifically the blue-wing—can last to mid-October.

Throughout the Eastern states, spin fishermen will have success year-round on the following lures in sizes from very small (0-size blades on spinners) to medium (Size 1 or 2 spinner blade, ½-ounce spoons).

Jerry Gibbs fly fishes on a section of northern New Jersey stream.

31

Spinners	Spoons
Mepps	Daredevle
Panther Martin	Miller Flutter Spoons
Abu Reflex	Ice Fishing Jigs and Spoons
C. P. Swing	
Rooster Tail	
Cotton Tail	

Plugs	Wobblers
Rapala	Phoebe
Rebel	

You and I have both caught trout on other lures in specific places. The above baits, however, are readily available throughout the area under discussion and they will take trout anywhere within the region as well as other areas. Silver, gold, red-and-white, with a little yellow trim are the only finishes you need. It is nice to have some of your spinners trimmed with buck or squirrel tail, however.

Natural-bait fishermen will find the common nightcrawler, or pieces of him, a superb bait early and late in the season, and after a mid-summer rainstorm. Preserved minnows sewn onto a hook, live minnows —especially alewives (locally called herring) in larger lakes—are consistent producers. Trout or salmon egg clusters early and late in the season are also excellent bait.

The choice of flies can be a nearly endless thing within this part of the country. I have certain favorites for particular waters, but if I needed to limit my selection drastically, I would not want to be without the following flies:

IMPORTANT EASTERN FLIES WITH APPROXIMATE EMERGENCE TIMES

Fly	Hook Sizes	Emergence Period
Quill Gordon	14, 16, 18	April–mid-May
Blue-wing Olive	18, 22, 24	April–mid-October
Hendrickson	12, 14, 16	April–late May
Trichoptera order (caddis flies). Fly: Adams tied in regular or spent-wing style.	14, 16, 18, 22	April–May, then sporadically throughout season in smallest sizes.
American March Brown	12, 14	Mid-May–mid-July
Light Cahill	14, 16	Mid-May–mid-August

Sulpher Dun	16, 18	May–July
Gray Fox	12, 14	May–mid-June
Large Mahogany Dun. Fly: Royal Wulff, Slate-wing Coachman, Slate Brown Paradun.	8, 10, 12	May–September
Green Drake (the Mahogany suffices in many places where the Green Drake has vanished)	8, 10	June
Tricorythodes. Fly: White-wing Black Caenis. Fly: White-wing Cream.	22–28	July–September

Of the above flies, patterns to imitate the dun (subimago) are in order for all but the Tricorythodes and Caenis. Use a spinner imitation. Spinner imitations for the Hendrickson, Light Cahill, Sulpher Dun, and Green Drake are also useful, but make sure you have the dun patterns.

I use nymphs of the Quill Gordon, Hendrickson, Light Cahill, Large Mahogany Dun (a fast swimmer), plus black-and-brown Woolly Worms a great deal.

For streamers I won't be caught without a Muddler Minnow, and a Marabou Muddler. I also recommend the following streamers: Mickey Fin, Black Nose Dace, White Marabou, Black Marabou.

Besides their obvious necessity on the limestone streams, late-season terrestrials are finding their way onto the end of my tippet more and more during the late season. I'd suggest that you round out your fly selection with some Jassids in green and dark colors; imitation grasshoppers, inchworms, shrimplike fuzzies like the Otter Shrimp, and both black and red ants.

There is much to be offered by the Eastern trout waters. The potential exists to take far larger trout than existed years ago, though the method for taking them may not be of your choosing.

Though some streams are forever lost, I feel others that were ruined in places over the past 50 or 75 years will be coming back—just like the anglers who have cut their fishing teeth in this part of the country. We may fish in the far wonderful places of the world, but still we keep returning for yet another time, to try the rivers, ponds and lakes that Eastern trout call home.

Float fishing for bass is a great pastime. These anglers are working one of Mississippi's freshwater coastal rivers for largemouth bass.

Catching Big Bass

BRUCE BRADY

My life is good and bass help to make it so. I caught my first bass in Mississippi as a lad of 7. By the time I was 10 I had traded a broken air rifle and half a pack of BB's for a short steel casting rod with no line guides and a Pflueger reel with no level wind.

My Mom wrapped on hairpin guides, and it wasn't long before my index finger and thumb served quite effectively as a level wind. I mowed lawns and paid for a crackleback Lucky 13 and a No. 2½ Hawaiian Wiggler. I began catching a few bass by the time I was 11, and by 12 my tackle was first-rate and I had whipped my first trophy largemouth, a thick 6-pounder that demolished an old silver flash Crippled Minnow I still have safely tucked away.

The Old Man once described the bream as the freckle-faced member of the fish family—the little brother with a hole in his britches and a smile on his face. How true!

And I believe it's just as true that the bass is the beer drinking, cigar chewing, fist-fighting old reprobate of the Finny Clan. He's a rough, tough, happy-go-lucky old battler—ready to wage a war if you'll just toe the mark. He's the Wallace Beery of the fish family.

My uncle Tut taught me the fundamentals of bass fishing. By today's standards I suppose he is an anomaly, though I shall always consider him to be a purist. He shunned the use of underwater lures, preferring to make his fish come to the top to take the plug. He favored 6-foot light-action rods by Heddon and True Temper. His reels were Pflueger Supremes and Shakespeare Presidents. His line was braided nylon and tested out at 9 pounds. It floated high and made it possible to transfer the spark of life from angler to surface lure, something imperfectly accomplished with monofilament lines.

Tut's favorite lures were Darters, Crippled Minnows, SOS's, the Diamond Lil' (she had rhinestones in her belly), and the venerable Dalton Special. With these plugs he was, and still is, an artist.

My uncle would not allow a landing net in his small cypress boat, pronouncing that all bass should be hand landed.

"The real test does not come until the fish is at the boat," he explained. "At this moment the fish has his best chance for escape. The line is short and tight and a powerful lunge at this instant will break it. If he can do it he has earned the right to freedom."

Small bass we could figure-8 at the side of the boat, sweeping them over the gunnel in one motion. Big fish had to be hand landed and there was some danger involved in this procedure. It depended on how they were hooked as to how we took hold. A fish hooked across the mouth had to be grabbed in the gills, while one hooked at the top or sides of the mouth could be grasped by the lower lip . . . with all the fingers if it was a large bass.

Tut's best bass weighed 12 pounds and when he planted his fist in its mouth the fish shook violently and buried two sets of treble hooks into the back of his hand. That was many years ago but he still carries the scars.

Because of Tut's techniques, he was considered not exactly divisible by 2 even in those long ago days. And we lost some fine fish as a result of his dogma. I recall one sunny spring day when we fished Buck Vernon's lake near our hometown. I was about 12 at the time and we had slowly worked our way along the shoreline, whipping our surface lures into the pockets of brush. We had taken several small bass. Tut released those he caught, while mine lazily trailed our boat on a cotton stringer.

By and by we approached a floating log which lay at a right angle to the bank, thereby creating a perfect hog hole. Tut gave me first cast and I put my lure deep into the recesses of the pocket, allowed the

Old oxbow lakes along the Mississippi River provide top bass fishing.

There's an art to hand-landing a big bass like this one Bruce Brady has grabbed. Note he's using all his fingers and not just the thumb and index finger.

ripples to die away as I had been taught, then gingerly nursed the plug outward.

Nothing happened and, when my cast was complete, Tut put his Diamond Lil' back into the same spot saying, "Sometimes an old bass will smack a bait he thinks is escaping."

With sharp jerks of the rod he sped his lure across the surface. Four feet from our boat a bass exploded on the lure, kicking up a wild geyser of spray. That savage strike is forever etched into my memory.

No sooner had the fish plunged downward than he came slashing through the top again. Tut had to give up some of his light line, of course, but by doing so he brought that long, whippy rod into the fight.

The third time the bass came up and angrily shook his head, he seemed to look at us to see who it was he fought. It was a helluva war he waged and he jumped uncommonly for so large a bass. Each time we thought he had settled in for the deep fight as bass will do, the line would rise and up he would come again, his thick body churning through the surface.

At last Tut had the fish on his side, gills flaring as he sucked for oxygen. Just at the side of the boat lay the end of that floating log and, just at the instant Tut reached to plant his big hand in that fish's mouth, he went down one last time taking the little line ino the jagged end of the log. The line popped and the fish was gone.

I sat unable to speak. Losing the fish after such a battle was an unthinkable thing to my young mind.

"He whipped me," Tut said at long last.

"If I'd had a net," I moaned, "I could have netted him twice."

Tut just smiled and shook his head.

Then we sat and talked about the fish and the battle. Tut seemed to me completely collected and I was amazed at his control. Then he got out a cigarette, lit it with his Zippo lighter, shook it as if shaking out a match, and calmly tossed it overboard! I stared in disbelief, then Tut realized what he had done and we both erupted into uncontrolled laughter.

But the real lesson I learned from that bass came a few minutes after we had resumed fishing. We had worked another 40 yards of cover when suddenly the bass came crashing through the top once again, shaking his head in a rage, the lure still dangling from his lip. Three times we watched him come up and on his third jump the plug sailed free. We both felt like applauding his demonstration of courage.

Trophy bass like this 10-pounder Bruce Brady is holding can be the catch of a lifetime. The bass is America's most popular freshwater game fish.

Bruce Brady, Pat Moore, and Paul Owens pose with a nice string of Alabama battlers taken near Brewton on surface lines. Bass fishermen have always been competitive.

Bass are super! They are omnivorous feeders. They will assault practically any fish including those almost their equal in size. They will devour frogs, crawfish, worms, salamanders, turtles, snails, ducklings, small eels, and even snakes.

A number of years ago Louisiana's Lake Larto was a favorite bass fishing lake of mine. We could judge how actively the bass were feeding simply by taking note of the cottonmouth moccasins draped in the trees and bushes near the water's edge. If snakes were gliding across the surface and not in the brush, we could accurately predict slow fishing for the day.

Largemouth bass fishing is available in every state today, with the exception of Alaska, and Old Bigmouth is the most popular of all the basses. In fact, bass fishing grounds are so numerous that we may only have room here to touch on a few of the better and more famous waters.

All of the Florida lakes and rivers are prime coverts for bass. Lake Jackson, Lake Kissimmee, and the St. Johns River are noted for their very large fish. Most of the really big bass are, incidentally, taken on live shiners.

Lake Eufaula, lying along the border between Georgia and Alabama, is certainly one of the nation's top bass lakes.

Both Mississippi and Louisiana can boast of hundreds of ancient oxbow lakes along the Mississippi River, as well as many hot, new reservoirs like Mississippi's Ross Barnett and Louisiana's Toledo Bend.

Texas has good bass water in virtually all sections. Oklahoma, Arkansas, Tennessee, and Kentucky all have numerous river systems interlaced with huge flood-control and power company impoundments.

Reservoirs in New Mexico, Arizona, and California produce very fine bass, and some anglers are predicting a new world's record largemouth will eventually come from a California lake. Other lakes in Oregon, Montana, and the Great Lake states can claim excellent largemouth bass fishing.

Smallmouth bass, to me, are like welterweight fighters. Old Bigmouth steps through the ropes with weight, power, and a haymaker right. But his smallmouth cousin brings you his speed, his timing, and a brutally quick left hand. I also believe they can out-think the largemouth.

Some of the more famous smallmouth waters include those in Maine and other New England states. Smallmouth fishing is also excellent in Ontario, Manitoba, and in the northern portions of the Great Lakes, especially in Lake Michigan and Lake Huron.

Fine smallmouth fishing is available in certain parts of the Midsouth, including such impoundments as Dale Hollow (home of the world's record 11-pound 15-ounce smallmouth), Wilson Lake, Center Hill, and Bull Shoals. The rivers and streams of the Ozark Mountains, as well as the impoundments along the TVA system, are all great smallmouth waters.

When I was a kid, the small rivers near home—the Homochitto, the Fair, McCalls, Bahala—all had long deep pools at every bend. These pools were interlaced with sandbars that gleamed white in the summer sun. That was before the forests were cleared away in large blocks as they are today, allowing the rivers to silt up and fill in the choice holes.

Well, in these little streams there dwelled a bass we called Redeyes. They are a small fish and a 3-pounder is a real lunker. And their eyes are, in fact, red. We knew these fish were bass but not the largemouth variety. Most folks were certain they were smallmouths (though their mouths were not small).

They are magnificent fighters for their size and skilled in the proper use of the current. They are delicious table fish. They are, in fact, Spotted Bass.

Most Redeye fishermen in those old days used canepoles and baited with minnows, worms, and small crawfish. Some anglers were able to realize the full value of these scrappers and took them with fly rods and small flies. Black Gnats and Peck's Bass Killers were favorites.

Spotted Bass found in Alabama, Mississippi, Georgia, South Carolina, Tennessee, and Virginia are known as the Coosa variety. The world's record Redeye weighed 6½ pounds.

Kentucky Spotted Bass range extends from the Gulf Coast states northward to Illinois, and stretches from North Carolina westward to Kansas and Nebraska. The world's record for this species weighed 8 pounds 10 ounces, and was caught in Alabama's Lewis Smith Lake in 1972. Subspecies of the Spotted Bass include the Sewannee, Wichita, and Redeye.

"Spots" are native to the small crystalline streams of their range. Small surface lures and spinner baits are effective spot producers. While spots seldom weigh more than two pounds, many a fisherman has been fooled by the fight of these bantamweights into thinking he has latched onto a lunker fish.

During my lifetime I have witnessed and taken part in a bass fishing revolution. Perhaps the two most important influences in this revolution have been the introduction of the plastic worm as an artificial bait, and the use of electronic depth sounders to reveal concentrations of bass around deep-water cover and bottom contours.

Only a few years ago we located deep-water hotspots by trolling deep running lures—one of the dullest pastimes known to man.

But experience has taught us that bass spend the majority of their time in these deep haunts, migrating periodically into the shallows and other productive feeding areas. Hydrographic maps aid in the location of these sanctum sanctorums.

Oxygen meters and thermometers reveal optimum water conditions, allowing us to quickly eliminate unproductive areas and to concentrate our efforts where fish populations are highest.

Twenty years ago the johnboat was standard with bass fishermen in the Deep South. Any outboard motor larger than a 10-horse was considered excessive and dangerous. Now, I am equipped with a large and fast bass boat. A foot-controlled electric trolling motor has replaced the short sculling paddle I once used. I have electric anchor hoists, automatic bailers, and padded swiveling Captain's chairs.

The long, whippy rods of yesterday have been replaced with shorter rods having fast tip action. I own stiff-action worm rods such as Browning's new graphite model with which the slightest touch of the bait is telegraphed through the line and into my hands. I have free-spool casting reels and stout monofilament lines. I also find fly-fishing tackle and spinning outfits useful and productive from time to time.

I suppose over the years I have lost a part of the purity of style

Many modern day bass fishermen fish from bass boats such as this one which features all the comforts of home. Note the electronic depth finder above the instrument panel. These are great big water craft.

Uncle Tut passed along to me. I use a net now (Tut still does not). I use an almost infinite variety of lures, including a wide selection of underwater types (Tut still does not). I still prefer to take my fish on top, but I realize I can catch many, many more fish on sub-surface lures. I know that deep-water fishing can produce a heavy stringer of bass while throwing a surface lure may not produce a single strike during the same period of time.

I believe all of these innovations are good. They broaden our horizons, they maintain our interest, and, most important of all, they help us catch fish. And still all of this paraphernalia isn't essential to produce a good mess of bass.

"Points and coves," Tut said. "That's where you should spend most of your fishing time."

I recall a summer's day years ago when that advice stood me in good stead. I was fishing Lake Sebago for smallmouths and I had no depth finder, oxygen meter, nor plastic worms. I did have a good selection of plugs and spoons. I concentrated my efforts on the narrow little points and shady coves and I took a nice string of fish.

Brushy pockets like this one make perfect homes for bass.

Once, on the St. Lawrence River, I found my fish among the rocks off a point almost beneath a town bridge. A spoon and pork rind was trump. If I could fire my lure into the rocks, let it settle a moment, then bring it briskly out just right, one of the Canadian bronzebacks would hammer it.

I remember an August day on Black Lake when I had fished hard all morning for one bass. Back at the dock Jack Bonn told me, "If you want a mess of bass go anchor in the open water where Workmans Bayou comes into the lake. Throw toward the point on your left and get your plug down deep."

I took Jack's advice and strung seven bass in short order. Later I learned there was a very nice drop-off out from that point. Jack had located that deep water sanctuary with a lead line and some hard work.

The Bass, bless his old heart, has remained the same all through the years. But the sport of bass fishing, alas, has changed enormously in recent times. Gentlemen, we can no longer buy Heddon Go-Deeper Crabs off the shelves of our favorite sporting goods shops. And lots of water has gone through the old spillway since those warm summer evenings when anglers competed for nothing more than a feeling of satisfaction or at most a cold beer on the way home.

Today, it is often a run for the money from the initial command, "Gentlemen, start your engines," until the final weigh-in when the payoff is in dollars and cents.

Like so many mushrooms, bass clubs have sprung up all over the country. Competition is vigorous among club members as well as with other clubs in other towns and other states. Professional bass fishing tournaments often cop the headlines on sport pages across the land.

As for myself, I have mixed emotions about these excursions into professionalism. It's not the competition that disturbs me, for bass fishermen have always scrapped each other. I grew up among some bass fishermen who learned to cast with their handles up when F.D.R. was President. These guys . . . Tut Brady, Happy Robertson, Paul Sartin, Gene Neal, Doc Arrington, Bob Davis . . . were all fiercely competitive. They fished the lakes along The River and they fished to win, but the payoff was the winner did no cooking and the low man had to wash the dishes.

In mulling it over, I suppose these men did constitute a bass club of sorts. They shared ideas, they competed, and they were concerned about the Battler when fishing got slow. Still, it's not the same today and it could be we've lost something somewhere along the way.

Among the bass I've met through the years a few still burn bright in my memory. Twenty-five years ago Bob Stamps and I fished a nearby lake regularly. Late one spring, near sundown, I whipped a rainbow Dalton into a shadow-patterned pocket in the reeds. As the plug touched down, I saw the swirl and wake of a big bass roll past it. Quickly I began a series of sharp jerks of the rod tip that had the bait literally jumping across the surface.

As the lure cleared the pocket, a bass exploded into it, tearing the reel handles from my fingers. He barreled under our boat, the power of his rush bringing my line into the corner of the hull. When the line went taut it snapped. At the same instant the fish jumped on the off side of the boat not yet aware he was already free.

At that time there lived in our little community a man whose proficiency with a six-shooter was well established. He was known by all as Bad Henry. Bob Stamps and I passed this moniker along to our newly found bass.

We took turns casting for that bass during the remainder of the spring and early summer. By actual count I hung him twice, once on a Dalton Special and once on a Black Jitterbug. Bob tied into him on one occasion with a Crippled Minnow and again with a lure called "The Ding-Bat." Each time the fish managed to tear off or break the line. We both judged him to weigh 9 or 10 pounds.

But, alas, one day Bad Henry didn't answer the bell. We never did battle with him again. I don't know if he died of the wounds we gave him, or if he simply declared himself Champ and followed some young and shapely female away to some other part of the lake. He was a great fish.

Moonlit nights are lovely times to go bass fishing. They are also highly productive times, especially if there is much daylight activity on the lake, such as waterskiing and similar activities of dubious value.

One of my favorite night-fishing lakes is Louisiana's Lake St. John. One moonlit night I approached a great moss-draped cypress, its roots extending into the depths like the fingers of a giant hand. I was casting a black spinner bait with trailer hook and pork rind. Carefully

I put the lure across the lambent patterns of moonlight and began a slow retrieve that would take the lure deep.

As the big spinner flashed alongside the trunk something stopped the bait cold. I put the steel to it, uncertain whether I had hooked a root or a bass. I made several quick turns of the reel handle and slowly the line began to swing to the left and to rise. Then a huge bass vaulted through the surface in a shower of moonlight and water. It was a sight to remember.

For 5 minutes I wrestled with him. He didn't jump again. Twice I was forced to give line when I thought the tension was nearing the breaking point. I was almost convinced I would land him when suddenly the hooks pulled out and it was all over. He was a magnificent bass.

There are others carefully tucked away in my memory. Bass are like women in this respect. It seems to be the ones you didn't get that are most fondly remembered.

Moonlit nights are lovely and productive times to fish for bass. Hand landing fish at night is a risky business.

Pete Mullikin works bass holding cover in Mexico's Lake Guerrero near Victoria. Bass fishing there is fabulous.

Bruce Brady hefts a few of the many bass he caught on Mexico's Lake Guerrero. Paddler holds up 6-pounder. Mexico has the best bass fishing in the world at this time.

Perhaps the finest bass fishing in the world is now taking place in Mexico. Big, new impoundments such as Dominquez, Obregon, and Guerrero have amazed the angling world with their bass productions.

A month ago some friends and I fished Lake Vincente Guerrero near Ciudad Victoria in the state of Tamaulipas. We were the guests of Ron Speed of Forney, Texas, who operates S & W Hunting and Fishing Service, the only camp on the bank of the lake at that time.

Weather conditions were terrible the first day out, and though we fished hard we took few bass. But the following day the weather was beautiful and the bass action was unbelievable. I lost count of the fish I caught. I changed lures a dozen times. I took bass on top, on shallow runners, medium runners, and on deep-diving plugs. In short, I failed to find a lure the bass would *not* hit!

Nowadays, however, it isn't necessary to travel great distances to find good bass fishing waters. In fact, some of the finest bass fishing is readily available in nearby farm ponds. There are several million of

This is a good selection of deep diving plugs, spinners and spoons. The plastic worm has had great impact on modern day bass fishing.

Surface lures such as these are fun to fish. They can be deadly in the hands of an expert. Braided lines are best for fishing surface plugs.

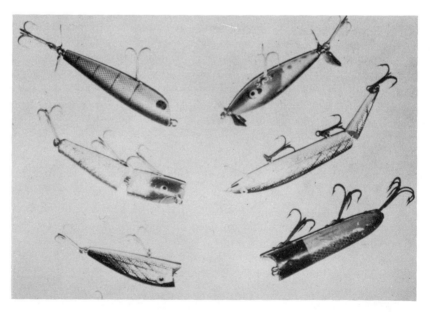

these little lakes scattered about the country (there are more than 150,000 in my home state of Mississippi). With permission from the owner, anglers can test their abilities whether they are top-water men or plastic-worm experts.

As I mentioned at the start of this chapter, I caught my first big bass near home when I was 12. My son took his first trophy bass, an 8½-pounder, when he was 8 years old. He hooked this fish on a purple worm in 20 feet of water, but he did it by himself without any help from his old man.

I can still see the tip of his tongue at the corner of his mouth as he fought and won a battle which by all counts he should have lost. I also remember the prayer I uttered when the big fish came busting through the top.

My last big bass was taken a week ago. I made him come up and take a surface lure. He fought well and when he was whipped I hand landed him. He tipped the scales at 7 pounds.

The bass may lack some of the beauty of a rainbow trout, the flavor of a walleye, and the strength of a musky, but he has a portion of all these fine qualities—plus something special which makes him No. 1.

You know, for those of us old enough to remember, there was something just right about the way Sugar Ray threw a left hook. And Glenn Miller's band had a special sound when they played "Moonlight Serenade." And today it's just as true that O. J. Simpson has a spark the other running backs can't match. Old Elvis has an excitement about him other performers cannot equal.

And so it is with the Battler. He is cunning, he is raging, he is wild. He is something special and he's destined to rule the freshwater world for a long, long time to come.

Pictured here is a good selection of bass lures. The spinner baits can be fished both shallow and deep.

The instant the mate touches the leader, a marlin explodes skyward in a final bid for freedom. Billfish are among the most spectacular fish in the sea because of the way they stalk a skipbait and their performance when hooked.

Fishing
the Offshore Waters

MARK SOSIN

Like the irresistible song of a siren, the seemingly endless expanse of blue water that parallels our coastlines continues to lure a growing army of anglers seaward where the many moods of restless oceans are as invigorating to the soul as the challenge of countless gamefish species. Probing and prowling the spray-capped swells beyond the sight of land once remained solely within the province of the affluent angler who could ignore the costs of expensive hulls and their upkeep and concentrate on fishing skills and techniques. Today, all that has changed. Smaller and faster boats with unbelievable seaworthiness for their size race for the horizons from ports everywhere, carrying determined anglers of every persuasion.

For years, the uninitiated referred to this offshore sport as "deep sea fishing," a misnomer that instantly labeled the user of this term as a hinterlander who was a stranger in outrigger country. Many inshore and interior fishermen received their baptism aboard a charter craft that catered to tourists. Crews mechanically performed the necessary functions and, even though the angler in question managed to boat perhaps the largest fish he had ever seen, he never really appreciated what he

Trolling is the primary technique in offshore waters and this boat is typical of those that chase gamefish on all our coasts. Outriggers are used to spread the baits and to offer an instant dropback in the case of billfish.

missed. Most of the excitement in blue-water sport comes from locating and baiting the quarry on tackle that is equal to the task. Jumping in a well-designed fighting chair and being harnessed to an outfit that is too heavy in the first place with a fish already on the other end leaves something to be desired and robs the angler of the real thrills.

The price of offshore gamefish is eternal vigilance. It is not always easy to remain alert (much less awake) when the monotonous drone of engines fills your ears and the unceasing swaying of a boat rocks your body like the rhythmic movement of a giant cradle. Yet, if you expect to catch fish, you must work at it and resist the temptation to doze off or become lackadaisical. Even aboard a charter craft with an efficient skipper and mate, you'll reap far more enjoyment if you train your eyeballs on the skipbaits and watch for signs of an approaching fish.

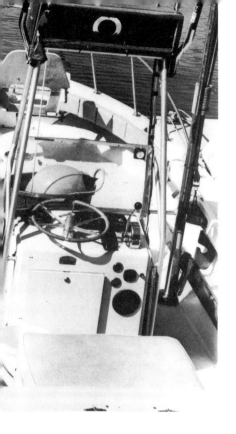

Small, fast, center-console boats are now being used on the offshore grounds. Note how the fighting chair has been rigged in the bow to enable this smaller craft to follow a fish rather than having to back down. Outriggers are above the center-console and the depth sounder is mounted high so it can be seen easily.

Trolling is the primary technique for exploring the offshore grounds because it enables a boat to cover the largest area in the shortest possible time. It is also the one method that is effective on most species of gamesters. Natural baits rigged either to swim just under the surface or skip on top are the favored offerings and the type you use is normally dictated by where you are fishing. On the West Coast, for example, the flying fish is a favorite, but across the continent you'll discover that balao, mullet, and squid receive preference. White marlin anglers sometimes use eels and blue marlin aficionados may drag a whole mackerel. There are other baits, of course, but these are the standards.

Big-game fishermen are recognizing more and more how important it is to rig a bait properly. Care in preparing an offering can make a difference in the number of strikes. There are several publications that picture the procedure for rigging various baits and, if you are a new-comer to the scene, it would pay for you to study them as well as en-list the aid of more experienced hands. Once you learn the technique, it's easy. You can keep offshore baits in a freezer until they are needed. Let them thaw naturally or in a bucket of salt water. Fresh water can cause these baits to spoil before you ever put them overboard. Whenever possible, an ample supply should be rigged before the boat leaves the dock or no later than on the way to the fishing area. When the action starts, it's too late to rig or sew a bait.

To be effective, an offshore bait must be fresh and it must swim cor-rectly. It is poor economy to try to get by with a mutilated squid or balao. After each strike, it pays to change the bait even if it appears to be in good shape. You can always save it for later in case you run out. Before streaming any bait, hold it in the water alongside the transom and watch its action. If it spins in the water, it is rigged in-correctly. You can often remedy the malfunction by bending the bait back and forth to break or soften the backbone and by enlarging the cavity where the hook sits. Successful anglers don't want to waste even a single minute with a bait that isn't going to catch fish.

There is no standard way to set a cockpit for trolling, but there are several guidelines that will help. Most boats rigged for this kind of sport have a pair of outriggers that can be extended outward on either side to help spread the lines. Lightweight 'riggers are now available for the small, center-console craft that are being pressed into offshore service.

Larger boats generally fish four lines: one from each outrigger and two directly over the transom (known as flat lines). It makes more sense to stream the outrigger lines farther back and to fish the flat lines closer aboard. Distances vary with personal preference and the species you seek, but we can strike an average. Outrigger lines should be fished from 75 feet to 125 feet astern. The flat lines will produce from 40 to 60 feet behind the boat, but there are some species that will charge a bait right up to the transom.

The important point to remember is that a trolling set-up is not static. Throughout the day, you should adjust the length of each line until you hit the combination that works. At the same time, you can switch baits between rods or change offerings. Blue-water fishing is a game of experimentation. The greatest failing most anglers have is

*Modern sportfishing boats are a maze of electronic equipment and special-
ized gear for taking gamefish. Here, the skipper operates the boat from a
tuna tower, giving him a superb panorama of the baits behind the boat and
the whole ocean. He can often see fish behind the baits from this perch
that are not visible to anglers in the cockpit.*

complacency: the willingness to drag the same baits in the same position at the same speed and the same distance astern forever and ever.

There are a few other theories worth discussing. The basic approach
is to use the smallest bait that will readily bring a strike from the
species you seek. The reason is simply that it will be easier for a fish
to swallow and that means a better chance of hooking your quarry. On
rough days, you should use slightly larger baits and more swimming
baits in the spread (instead of skipping baits). The purpose of this
change is that it is more difficult for fish to spot skipbaits (and particularly small ones) among the spray from whitecaps. You might, for

example, try two skipbaits and two swimmers when it's dusty going instead of a combination of three skipbaits and one swimming bait.

Veteran offshore anglers often use hookless teasers to attract gamefish behind the boat. Everything you can imagine has been used at one time or another, ranging from Coke bottles to baseball bats to garbage pail lids, and they all work. The marketplace, however, offers a selection of specially designed teasers that have proven themselves at sea. Most are made from a molded plastic head with a skirt of nylon, Saran, or even strips of vinyl. Others have wood heads and there are a few that are turned on a lathe completely from a hunk of hardwood. Behind a boat, these teasers do everything but whistle and go through a ritual of skipping, diving, swerving, and splashing.

Teasers are a personal thing and once you find one that works for you, it pays to hang onto it. Some will raise more fish than others, so treat a favorite with respect. There are also soft teasers made in the shape of squid or baitfish that can be towed. Lately, a number of anglers are rigging these artificial squids in tandem with as many as half a dozen in the daisy chain. They'll raise their share of fish.

Though promoted by billfishermen, teasers are by no means limited to sails and marlin. Many other species will charge a teaser and, if you are alert to see the action, you can swing a natural bait over and pick up the hungry denizen. Some billfish specialists claim that at least half the sails and marlin they raise will charge the teaser first.

Again, you have a choice in where you drag teasers. Some skippers prefer to work them low on the outriggers and control the distance from the bridge. Others merely tie handlines to the teasers, secure the lines to stern cleats, and toss the offerings over. If you drag teasers 35 to 50 feet astern, you'll be in the ballpark.

A setup with only natural baits and noisy teasers ignores many of the smaller species that can invade the churning turmoil behind a boat. Members of the tuna family often swarm in and out of a wake and, if there isn't a small enough offering for them to inhale quickly, they'll be gone in a matter of seconds. Anglers who specialize in billfish or giant tuna don't want to be bothered with other fish, but for most of us, these smaller denizens can break up the monotony of trolling and add excitement.

The old cure-all has been the Japanese feather—a small, chromed leadhead lure with sparse feathers. You rig your own by inserting wire

Teasers are another trick in the arsenal of the offshore angler. Some, like the top two, are trolled without hooks to attract fish. The third one can be used as an artificial lure by rigging it with a hook, while the plastic squid can be rigged either as a teaser or a lure.

Many offshore veterans insist on trolling a Jap feather or one of the new plastic lures for smaller species that might invade the wake of the boat.

or mono leader material through a hole in the head and then tying a hook on the end. Frequently, Jap feathers are trolled in tandem with two or three jammed together. They really work, but, unfortunately, the good ones are hard to locate in tackle shops. Local imitations have too many feathers and use a clear vinyl or plastic between head and feathers. The old type uses a material we have always called "fish skin" that is stiff when dry, but extremely pliable when wet.

A few American manufacturers have been making an array of small trolling lures. The best that I've seen come from Sevenstrand and they boast various shaped heads with skirts of plastic. My favorite colors are green-and-yellow, green-and-white, and red-and-white. Sevenstrand also makes skirts of this plastic that can be slipped over natural baits to add appeal. Both the skirts and the lures are available in a number of sizes and you can select those best suited to your fishing area. Regardless of where you pursue your sport, however, it pays to carry a supply aboard your boat or in your tackle box.

In the early days, offshore tackle developed through modifications of existing gear and through the efforts of pioneers who designed equipment to meet the rigorous demands of larger fish. When the International Game Fish Association appeared on the scene as a record-keeping body, it also worked diligently to bring a sense of order to the tackle being used. The IGFA merely wanted to ensure that record holders enjoyed equal advantages or disadvantages, but its establishment of line classes carries over to this day. World records are kept on the basis of the breaking strength of the line and current categories are 6-pound-test, 12, 20, 30, 50, 80, 130, and unlimited.

All so-called regulation offshore tackle is based on these line classes. Rods are now designated by the line they are designed to handle and you'll find 20-pound rods, 50-pound rods, and rods for all of the other IGFA categories in most tackle shops catering to the offshore crowd. There was a time when the IGFA specified the length of the rod tip and the butt, but they now set minimums and maximums. The rod tip cannot be less than 50 inches and the butt cannot be more than 27 inches (curved butts are measured straight across from center of reel seat to tip of gimbal).

The standard trolling rod has a tip section about 5 feet long and an 18-inch butt. Heavier classes are a bit longer. The major differences, however, lie with the individual manufacturers. It is up to the maker to declare the class of his rods and the latitude is great. What one company calls a 30-pound rod would be a 20-pound outfit to another company and a 50-pound rod to a third manufacturer.

If there is a failing in commercially built rods, it is simply that they are rated too heavy. The breaking strength of the line should be the minimum limitation. Rods must be reasonably stout so that you can troll a reasonable-size bait without the stick buckling in half, set the hook on a fish, and have enough backbone to pressure your quarry. Rods with tips that are too soft deprive the user of the edge he needs to fish successfully.

Modern innovations include roller guides and tiptops that are touted to reduce wear on the line and eliminate a great amount of friction. Unfortunately, rollers don't always roll and, when they malfunction, they can cause line fray. Except when wire line is used, they are still a good choice on conventional trolling rods.

You'll find that machined reel seats instead of the stamped variety often are part of more expensive rods and it's one way you can tell that the maker is trying to use the best components. Originally, the butt sections were made from wood, but better rods today have either fiberglass or aluminum butts. Wood has its shortcomings and it can be broken much more easily than glass or metal.

Most offshore anglers (especially those on charter boats) miss out on the fun because they use tackle that is too heavy. If you think about it, the majority of all fish caught on the ocean weigh 100 pounds or less. The exceptions would be some sailfish, blue marlin, striped marlin, black marlin, swordfish, tuna, and sharks. You may hang a husky snapper or amberjack over a reef, but that's the exception. An average angler aboard a boat with a skipper who can handle the controls should be able to boat any 100-pound fish on a 30-pound outfit. If you had to limit yourself to a single rod and reel, make it a 30-pound rig and you'll enjoy the sport much more.

Charter skippers also know this, but their tackle takes such abuse and they cater to so many inexperienced anglers that they consider 50-pound tackle to be light and 80-pound as standard. One can't blame them because tackle is expensive, yet most patrons never fully benefit from the performance of the fish. Heavier gear has a place when marlin fishing, chumming for huge sharks, or trying to boat a giant tuna. With tuna, you need at least an 80-pound outfit, and often a 130-pound

Handling and boating a giant bluefish reguires teamwork and a skilled crew. This beauty is being lifted aboard with the aid of a ginpole. Unless fishing pressure eases, the bluefish tuna may be a species of the past.

rig. Otherwise, the strong heart of that great fighter can give out in the depths and you don't have enough rod to plane the brute topside.

Let me offer another thought. Unless an angler is strong and in his prime, there is a definite limit to the amount of drag the arms, legs, and back can withstand. Youngsters, ladies, and senior citizens expend more energy fighting the weight of the rod and reel than the fish. For them, a wiser choice would be lighter tackle.

There's another thought I would like to share with you. In the last two years, I have come to the conclusion that the present concept of trolling rods up to 30-pound class might not be the best. Roller guides, aluminum butts, machined reel seats, and other goodies add weight to the rod. There are new light tackle blanks on the market that are unbelievably light, yet equally strong with plenty of reserve power. They can be built with the blank running right through the reel seat to the gimbal and cork can be used for the grips. Instead of roller guides, the new aluminum oxide variety are super smooth and can really do a job.

If you want the flexibility of two-piece sticks for travel or storage, the new rods can be center ferruled, using the solid glass, male-female method. I have used them successfully in three oceans and shudder at the thought of ever going back to the old standard models. There are those who would argue that the reel seat might be a bit light or some other component may be a compromise, but hold one in your hand and I think you'll agree that you'd be willing to run the isolated risk for the pleasure of such lightness.

Trolling reels can be broken into two categories: those with drags adjusted by a starwheel and those in which drag tension is set with a sliding lever arm. The lever-arm reels are generally more expensive and constructed from heavy aluminum or an equally strong metal. They are stout and designed to take all the punishment a big fish can dish out. Some of the lever-arm reels have a built-in stop so that you can throw the reel into strike drag without looking. There is an override system that enables you to employ more drag when necessary. These reels are much more expensive than the simpler starwheel models.

Reels with the basic starwheel method of setting the drag have accounted for more than their share of fish and are still the best buy for the money. If you can afford one of the deluxe reels, so much the better—but you don't have to be ashamed of a Penn Senator.

Any reel requires periodic maintenance and it's always a good idea to carry a supply of extra drag washers in case those in the reel become glazed or get disfigured after hand-to-hand combat. Drag washers should never be oiled or lubricated unless they are made of leather. Composition cork drags can be refinished by rubbing a little neatsfoot compound on them and using an emery board or crocus paper to remove any glaze.

The system of cataloging trolling reels is a throwback to the old days. Most makers use the "O System" in which O stands for Ocean. The larger the number preceding the O, the larger the reel. A 6/0 reel is bigger than a 4/0 and a 9/0 has more size and line capacity than a 6/0. The reel you select must be predicated on the type of fishing you do. There are standards, and a 4/0 reel is the normal choice for a 30-pound outfit. A 6/0 reel would be used with 50-pound and a 9/0 reel with 80-pound. If you are trying to land a big marlin on 50-pound, you might choose a 7½/0 instead of a 6/0 to get more line capacity. Some anglers now prefer a 3/0 with 30-pound class for general fishing and a 4/0 only if they're going for something bigger than usual. It's a matter of personal preference.

A few manufacturers are finally changing their views and labeling, calling a reel a 30-pound model, 50-pound model, and so on. To my thinking, this is a step in the right direction and a point I've been arguing for many years. We have 30-pound line and a 30-pound rod. Why call a reel a 4/0?

Regardless of how far a fish may or may not run when hooked, each reel should be filled to capacity. There should be some room under the reel pillars, however, or you run the risk of piling the line on one side and having the reel jam. If you don't have the reel filled, you lose the advantage of retrieving an adequate amount of line for every crank of the handle. Speaking of retrieve ratios, you can get by with higher ones on lighter outfits, but when you try to pump a giant bluefin or attempt to drag a black marlin up from the depths, you need a smaller ratio approaching 3:1 or 2:1.

You can load your reel with either monofilament line or braided Dacron. There are advantages to both. Monofilament has a certain amount of stretch which means that it will be a little forgiving. You can make mistakes and still survive because this stretch will absorb the shock. Dacron doesn't have stretch and that means you can pump a fish better and set a hook with more authority. There are proponents of both types for all tackle, but the majority opinion would be to use monofilament up to 50-pound class and Dacron for 80- and 130-pound class. Fifty-pound is the pivot point and you can go either way. My own choice would be mono for 50-pound class and Dacron for above it.

The IGFA limits the length of the leader to 15 feet of any material plus 15 feet of double line for all classes through 50-pound. You may use 30 feet of leader and another 30 feet of double line with 80-pound and 130-pound class. The standard leader material for most offshore species is single strand wire. Braided aircraft cable is preferred for marlin and sharks. There is a growing trend toward the use of heavy monofilament for sailfish and other species because the mono seems to encourage more strikes than wire.

Newcomers to salt water gaze across open seas and wonder how there could possibly be any skill involved in locating gamefish. To these neophytes, it would appear that a boat should merely drag baits at random and all hands should keep their fingers securely crossed. It doesn't work that way. It's not the surface of the water, but what is beneath it that is important. The place to start is with a navigational chart of the offshore waters. Begin by looking for the 20-fathom curve and the 100-fathom curve (if it is within reach).

Gamefish, like all other animals, tend to follow an edge. That's where they find food and it gives them a sense of security. Anytime you see a point or a pocket in one of those curves, it's a good place to probe. You will also discover that any sudden rise or dropoff will harbor baitfish and you can be sure there will be gamefish around. On the waterfront, you'll hear these places referred to as humps, lumps, rocks, reefs, or whatever, but they are all distortions of the bottom.

Currents are another factor in finding fish. Some currents are local in nature and will carry bait fish, while others such as the Gulf Stream are actually rivers of moving water. The edges of a current are often much more productive than the interior of that current. The moving water draws additional water with it and there is an upwelling from the deep to replace the water that is carried off by the current. Nutrients are forced to the surface where they burst into bloom. Baitfish feed on the nutrients and the fish you are after forage on the baitfish.

Water temperature is equally important. Some species cannot tolerate chilly water and, even though the area is normally a good one, there might not be any fish because the temperature is below the minimum for the species.

There's a difference between merely dragging baits and successful trolling. Some skippers are content to steer a course for a distant cloud formation and hope that a fish invades the spread. That's really playing a long shot. The number of variables in finding fish are staggering, but the trick is to eliminate as many as possible. Start with the trolling speed. For most species, it pays to begin with the minimum RPM setting that will keep the baits skipping realistically. Then, as the day progresses, change the throttle frequently until you uncover a pattern. Some fish, such as members of the tuna family, want a fast-moving bait and, if you are only fishing for tuna, you can push the throttle ahead.

The vital factor is to always know where you are and what is beneath the hull. You might work along the edge of the 20-fathom curve for awhile and then zigzag across it, easing back and forth from deeper to shallower water and back to deeper. Try moving with the seas, against the seas, and across the seas. Billfish often swim with the swell and by crossing the seas.

Regardless of where you fish, most of the species will be migratory and, although an odd fish may be taken at any time of the year, most will be taken during certain months. White marlin appear off Ocean City, Maryland, from mid-June through mid-September. Blue marlin put in a major appearance off North Carolina in early June. There are also dolphin at that time of year off Hatteras. Tuna fishing gets better in late summer and early fall, with the exact dates varying by location.

School tuna this size are a rarity because of heavy pressure from commercial clippers coupled with increased catches by sport fishermen. At one time, they provided exceptional sport for both chummers and trollers along the Northeastern coast.

FISHING THE OFFSHORE WATERS

The same procedure is common to the Gulf Coast and the West Coast. Yellowtail, albacore, billfish, and other species follow a timetable off California and Baja. Recently, some of the long-range boats have been running to the Canyons at the edge of the Continental Shelf in the Atlantic and the Gulf of Mexico. Big-game fishing has been excellent in these waters, but it is a long trip and care must be taken to ensure safety. A sudden storm could prove disastrous to small craft caught 100 miles at sea.

If you are a visitor at a coastal port, a trip to the charter docks will

Shunned by billfishermen because of its tendency to crash a carefully rigged bait, the dolphin is one of the greatest gamefish in the sea for its size. It will strike virtually any bait or lure and you can hold a school around the boat while you cast to them with light gear.

Sailfish are found on all three coasts of the United States and are a perfect fish to take on light tackle. One should never use an outfit heavier than 30-pound class for any sail-fish.

bring you instant information on what is being caught offshore. If you have your own boat, local intelligence is easy to glean at dockside or from a tackle shop.

Offshore fishing to some specialists is more than trolling. An increasing number of anglers are taking casting gear to sea and using it on dolphin, small tuna, and even sailfish. The trick is to tease up your quarry with hookless offerings, stop the boat, and toss a lure or fly to the critter while it's trying to swallow a plastic squid or a hookless balao. You might not get a chance every day, but it's worth carrying the tackle just in case.

Reefs and rockpiles are known fish havens. Pelagic species are at the mid-depths, but there are also a host of husky bottom dwellers. Some fishermen enjoy the technique of deep jigging in which they drop a lead-headed bucktail to the bottom on plug-casting gear or spinning tackle and then work the lure to the surface. This method can be deadly and the number of species taken is staggering. You can lose a lot of fish on the light gear, but that's part of the fun.

Still another method of catching offshore fish is by chumming. In New England, this is the basic approach in tuna fishing. A slick of ground, chunked, and whole fish is dispatched over the side. Lines are sometimes kept aboard until tuna show in the slick and, on other occasions, a bait is floated out with a balloon as a bobber. Chumming works equally well over reefs or coral heads. You can either fish with natural bait in the slick or watch until fish appear and then cast artificial lures.

In Florida, kite fishing has been refined to an art. A special kite is flown from the boat and a live bait allowed to dangle on the surface below the kite. The boat is moved very, very slowly and almost any species of fish might explode without warning, but it is primarily a method of taking billfish.

The offshore options are only limited by one's imagination and inclination. It is a fascinating phase of the sport that requires total dedication and devotion to technique. The trout purist likes to bathe in the thought that his is a complicated sport. As foreign as blue water can be to a swift flowing trout stream, fishing for the heavyweights can be equally demanding on the anglers involved and there is just as much skill needed.

It is vital that all of us realize that the mysterious depths of the sea are not an endless well with an unceasing supply of gamefish. Very

Chumming can be an effective technique for tuna and over reefs or rockpiles in many parts of the sea. In some cases, gamefish follow the oily slick and, in others, baitfish feed on the chum and the predators feed on the baitfish.

little is known about marine species, but scientists do recognize that increased fishing pressure from both sport and commercial sources can virtually eliminate some stocks of fish. The bluefin tuna is a case in point. At this writing, this gallant gladiator is fighting for its very existence. Longlining of tuna and billfish has also had serious effects on the size of fish and the quantity.

To aid science in learning more about each species, anglers are frequently asked to cooperate by tagging billfish and tuna as well as other species. The results have helped researchers make serious inroads into the patterns of certain species and, by practicing conservation, we help to ensure the success of a species for generations to come.

Cohos like this one are rugged fighters. Handling them takes tackle and gear of the type shown.

The Coho Story

JOHN CARTIER

In April, 1966, I caught a 6-inch coho salmon in Michigan's Platte River. The tiny fish was one of 850,000 fingerlings planted that same month as an experiment by the Michigan Department of Natural Resources. The coho was hooked by accident while I was fishing for steelhead trout. I gently released the salmon and wondered if he'd grow up.

Sixteen months later I hooked my second coho. He slammed a silver wobbling plug in the blue-green water of Lake Michigan, 4 miles offshore near the city of Manistee. He tore up the surface of the big lake with a fighting frenzy. After many minutes of battle I was the excited winner. My trophy was as silver as a new-minted dime, and he weighed 14½ pounds. He was one of the original planting of fingerlings, and he'd grown over 14 pounds in 16 months. Fantastic? That's only part of the story of ever greater coho fishing in the Great Lakes.

At dawn that morning, I wondered what I was getting into. Going out on the huge expanse of Lake Michigan in a 17-foot boat is cause for excitement in itself. It was the first day of September, 1967, but it was a cold, foggy, eerie morning.

There were three of us. Warren Holmes had trailered his boat from his home in North Muskegon to Manistee Lake. At 50, he's a veteran fisherman and he specializes in trolling Michigan trout lakes. George

Dorrell has been fishing the better part of his 58 years. The three of us, all family men, have shared many outdoor experiences.

Warren had previously rented dock space for his boat. We arrived at the dock just as daylight became a promise. Fog hung over the area like a blanket of smoke. We loaded our gear into the boat with an assist from the yellow beams of headlights on Warren's station wagon. Then we snapped off the lights and shoved off onto Manistee Lake.

We motored ½ mile up the shoreline then turned into the channel routing through the city of Manistee, and out into Lake Michigan. We weren't alone. Dozens of boats were ghosting through the fog. All were moving up the channel, all heading for the salmon grounds a couple of miles away.

When we passed the Manistee Coast Guard Station the foghorn at the end of the harbor pier moaned with ear-hurting repetition. Then we were on Lake Michigan. Warren gunned his 40-horsepower outboard and we cruised over gently rolling swells. The sun, just topping the horizon, showed as a huge, red ball behind slowly dispersing fog. With increasing visibility, we looked out on an amazing sight.

"Look at that!" George exclaimed. "Look at the boats. They're everywhere. There are hundreds of 'em out here."

Boats, from outboards to luxury cruisers, fanned out from the harbor entrance. "Well," Warren grinned, "we're here. I wonder how we go about catching a salmon?"

"We'll experiment," George answered. "Let's troll different types of rigs in different depths of water. We've got plugs and spoons and big streamers. Let's try everything."

Our discussion was probably typical of those in the boats around us. Information about runs of adult salmon in Lake Michigan was nil. This was the first time in history that full grown salmon had been in the lake. Did many fingerlings from the 1966 plantings survive? If so, did they really grow into 10- to 20-pound lunkers? If they did, were prespawning concentrations building off river mouths as predicted by fisheries biologists?

In late August, newspaper sport pages had headlined that the dream was true. The word spread like wildfire. By Labor Day weekend, when Warren, George and I got into the act, Michigan salmon were promoting the greatest concentration of fishermen ever assembled in the Midwest. An estimated 3,000 fishermen's boats suddenly peppered the shoreline waters between Manistee and Frankfort.

THE COHO STORY

By 9 A.M. the fog had been burned away by a bright sun riding in a blue sky. It was a calm day on the big water, perfect in every respect except fishing action. We weren't the only luckless anglers. Though we kept a watch on other boats we didn't see anybody hook or land a salmon.

"Maybe we're fishing too shallow," Warren guessed. "Let's turn north and troll up the shoreline."

An hour later we were 3 miles north of the harbor, 1 mile out from shore, and still fishless. Right after that George noticed something that had escaped our attention.

"Hey," he said, "look off there to the northwest. There's a group of boats out there on the horizon."

"Yeah," exclaimed Warren. "Now I think we've got something going. Those people aren't 4 miles out in the lake to get a sunburn. I'll bet they've found some salmon."

It took us a while to troll out there. As we neared our destination I glanced back at the main groups of boats closer to shore. They appeared as tiny specks in the distance. "Maybe we're too far out," I said. "I doubt if. . . ."

George chopped off my words with a lusty bellow. "I got one! Look at him go."

I whirled toward the stern. A second before George had been sitting in an aluminum lawn chair. He'd had his feet propped on the boat's gunwale. He'd had the butt of his rod resting on the chair seat, and he'd had the tip pointing straight up in the air. He'd been totally relaxed. All of that changed with the suddenness of an exploding bomb.

George went out of that chair as quickly as if someone had jabbed him with a pin. Now he was half-kneeling half-standing in the back of the boat. His 7-foot glass spinning rod was bent nearly double and the drag of his open-face reel was singing like a buzz saw. Behind the boat, 40 yards away, a great silver shape was walloping the surface of the water into a series of glistening eruptions of spray.

George wasn't fighting that salmon, he was just hanging on. Warren didn't get so excited. He'd fought many big trout from this same boat, and he knew exactly what to do.

"Throw the throttle in neutral," he warned me. "Get your line in."

I jabbed the throttle into position, then frantically reeled in my line. Warren already had his rod tucked away in the bow. He folded the two aluminum chairs, shoved tackle boxes and a minnow bucket under the stern decking, inspected the boat and said, "Okay, George, you've got all the room you need. Take your time, I want a close-up view of a salmon."

"He's running straight away," George blurted. "I haven't got much line left. Chase him. Hurry up!"

I shoved the throttle forward, but I shoved it too hard. The boat jumped ahead. Then George was yelling again. "He's turning, slow down!"

I was aware of my error almost as soon as I made it. I corrected our speed, then George began handling his salmon with the skill of a man who had hooked big fish before. And he did the job with a bass-action spinning rod, an open-face reel, and 10-pound monofilament.

Ten minutes later George worked his fish within 10 yards of the boat. We thought the battle was over. The salmon was just under the surface and we could see him in that sparkling water as clearly as if we were looking through a window. Warren reached for his landing net, then that salmon changed his mind. He suddenly blitzed broadside like a torpedo.

I've seen line slice water before, but I'd never seen it slice fast enough to throw spray. That's exactly what happened as the salmon peeled 20 yards of monofilament from George's reel in split seconds. The fish just about killed himself with that run. After it was over George brought his trophy to the boat with little trouble. Warren slipped his landing net under the hook-nosed slab of silver, then heaved it aboard.

"Whew," he grunted, "that's a lot of fish to handle in this net. Congratulations, George, you're now a salmon fisherman."

I guessed the lunker's weight at 13 pounds. George didn't commit himself, but he did say, "That's too much fish to put on a bass stringer. We'll have to use the boat's bow line. This is the first time in my life I ever used a ¼-inch rope for a stringer."

Five minutes later we were trolling again. There wasn't any listless attitude now. We were as alert as pointing dogs. It was seemingly impossible that another fish could take us by surprise, but that's exactly what happened.

We hadn't been back in business more than 30 minutes when Warren said, "Fish on in that boat ahead of us." By now we had trolled into the group of a couple dozen boats and the excited anglers ahead of us were less than 100 yards away.

We watched the fellow in the stern of the outboard work his fish for a long time. He did a good job, and eventually we saw the salmon splash close to the side of the small boat. Then, in amazement, we watched the happy angler shove his arm into the water.

"Bad news," I groaned, "those guys don't have a landing net. They'll never get that fish."

Warren pushed his trolling rod into a rod-holder clamped to the side of our boat. Then he cupped his hands, and was about to yell something to the man with the problem. The words never materialized, because at that instant Warren's rod tip whipped backward and his star-drag casting reel began whining.

"Fish!" I yelled. "Your rod, Warren. Get him!"

All of that was unnecessary. Warren had already jumped into action. He yanked the rod from the holder, reefed it upwards, and leaned backward. "He's still on," Warren grunted. "He's headed nonstop for Wisconsin. Man, they're runners."

This salmon didn't jump, but he put on a display of power just as remarkable. He surfaced with his green back out of water, then he streaked across the top of Lake Michigan with unbelievable speed. He blitzed straight away, reversed his direction, then angled off in another sizzling run. One moment Warren was winding furiously to take in slack line, the next moment he was straining to hold his bucking rod.

That's the way the battle went for 10 minutes, but Warren won it. George eventually slipped the net under the fish and salmon No. 2 swished over the boat's gunwale.

"Hey, Cartier," Warren quipped happily, "you haven't been doing anything except standing around. Did that guy in the other boat ever land his fish?"

"Darn if I know," I laughed. "I don't even see the boat anymore. That was a long time ago."

So was that trip a long time ago. I've been involved with scores of salmon trips on Lake Michigan since, but I'll never forget that first adventure because it was so unbelievable. During that day I discovered the fact that has shot up the blood pressure of hundreds of thousands of anglers since. For a guy who used to consider a 5-pound pike or bass a whopper, it's pretty much of a shock to realize that 10-pound salmon can be easy to catch, and that they're readily available.

When I made that first trip the good fishing was limited to the small fraction of Lake Michigan in the Manistee area. Now the action takes place along most of the big lake's shoreline in Wisconsin, Illinois, Indiana and Michigan. And it isn't limited to September. The fishing starts in April in the southern part of the lake which holds the warmest water at that time of year. Salmon winter in the warmest water they can find.

As spring matures the cohos begin moving north. They continue migrating until they arrive in the general area of their home stream, the stream in which they were planted as fry. This is when the top fishing blossoms because by this time the cohos weigh up to 15 pounds or more, they're concentrated in schools, and they go on feeding binges just prior to their spawning runs.

At this time, usually beginning about late August, you can be almost positive about getting in on the type of action I described. Why positive? Because there are many more salmon now, techniques for catching them have been refined, and the hotspots have been established. All of this excitement had its beginning in the early 1960's.

At that time Michigan fisheries biologists were studying the coho as a possible new sport fish for introduction into the Great Lakes. The end of the sea lamprey menace was in sight. The lamprey, a blood-sucking parasite, had decimated the big fish populations of the Great Lakes during the 1950's. After years of effort, a selective poison was developed that would kill lampreys, but would not harm fish.

Successful use of the poison greatly reduced lamprey populations in Lake Michigan. Now a new problem faced the biologists; how to elevate the depleted fisheries resource to its greatest potential for recreational fishing, and how to produce a maximum number of big fish in a hurry.

The challenge of adapting the coho to fresh-water environment became an intriguing possibility. Nowhere in the world had the species been permanently established outside its native range.

The coho, or silver salmon, is native to the Pacific Ocean from Monterey Bay, California, north around the Gulf of Alaska, and down the Asiatic Coast to the Japanese Islands. The salmon spawns in fresh-water streams in the fall of its third year of life, then it dies. Growth of cohos is phenomenal. In the Pacific area, they increase in size from less than 1 ounce to an average weight of 9 pounds in an 18-month period. Individual Western cohos have achieved adult weights of over 20 pounds.

THE COHO STORY

Cohos are dependent on stream reproduction. Fingerlings migrate to the sea (in this case, to Lake Michigan) after one year in the river. They wander over considerable distances while growing to adult size, then a very strong homing instinct urges them back to the parent stream when they are ready to spawn.

The cold, clear, deep waters of upper Lake Michigan were evaluated as ideal coho habitat. Lake Michigan was full of alewives; a small, silvery fish offering salmon an unlimited food supply. But, could young cohos (for the initial plantings) be produced in hatcheries? The answer was an emphatic yes. Everything about the coho seemed made to order for the Great Lakes.

In the spring of 1966, 850,000 yearling coho salmon were released in three Michigan rivers. The Platte and Manistee rivers in the Lower

Coho angling is at least a two-man job. Handling motor, fighting and landing fish is best accomplished by teamwork.

Peninsula received a total of 660,000. The Big Huron River, in the Upper Peninsula, received the balance of 190,000. The eggs for those releases were provided by the Oregon Fish Commission, and the fry were reared in Michigan hatcheries.

By fall of that year, the news was encouraging. Fishermen began catching a few jacks (early maturing males) in the rivers where they were originally planted. Large numbers of returning jacks were trapped in state DNR weirs on these same rivers. The 3- to 6-pound fish were healthy and fat. The experiment now looked as if it might pay off far beyond anyone's expectations.

By September, 1967, the coho success story was making history. Many anglers who had never seen a salmon were now catching them along the harbor towns on the northeast coast of Lake Michigan. It seemed as if 10-, 12-, 15-, and even 20-pound salmon had suddenly appeared out of nowhere.

With that beginning, more and larger plantings of cohos were placed in Lake Michigan, Lake Superior and Lake Huron. Lake Michigan got most of the fish because it is most suited as top coho habitat. By 1970, the lake was being planted with nearly 3 million tiny cohos annually. How many cohos are in the lake now is anybody's guess, but there are enough to rank Lake Michigan now as one of the 10 top freshwater fishing lakes in America.

Coho fishing is no longer the hit-and-miss adventure I mentioned at the beginning of this chapter. Fishing techniques have been refined, tackle specifically developed for Great Lakes salmon fishing is readily available, and the mysteries of where the cohos go and when they can be caught have been solved.

The hooking of a coho on Lake Michigan is not a test of skill. It's more a matter of knowing where to fish. Drag most any type of lure through a school of cohos and you'll likely find action. Of course it's true that some lures work better than others at given times of day in given areas. It's also true that these fish—being migratory—may be here today and gone tomorrow. Such problems are part of the challenge of fishing anywhere for any species, but they have been licked to a great degree in coho fishing.

The reason is that much of today's fishing is provided by charter-boat operators. These guys don't stay in business unless they know where the fish are and how to catch them. The good ones fish every day during the season whether they have paying charters or not. Charter-boat operators exchange information with each other on all phases of the fishing. It's a cooperative effort among experts.

So, if you want to learn how to catch cohos, your best bet is to pay for a charter trip for two. You'll learn more tricks of the trade in a day with an expert than you'd learn on your own in a month. Not only will you discover what works but you'll discover why it works, and that is the kind of knowledge it takes to catch fish.

With that experience you'll be able to go it on your own as to what type of fishing tackle and equipment to buy and how to use it. In general, though, there are some thoughts to keep in mind on tackle. Most experts go with rods in the 6½-foot category, the type called ocean-fishing or tournament rods. In medium-action, these rods are tops for handling cohos. Levelwind reels with a reliable drag and a spool capable of holding 200 yards of line get the nod along with heavy-duty spinning reels. There are few snags in Lake Michigan, so there is no reason to go beyond 20- or 25-pound-test lines. Such lines, used by skillful fishermen, will handle any coho with ease.

The most important equipment item to consider is the size and reliability of your boating equipment. Lake Michigan can get wild with sudden storms. It can kill people.

On September 23, 1967, a sudden lightning, wind, and rain storm ripped across the upper part of the lake. Twenty-foot waves materialized in moments. Thousands of fishermen trolling for cohos off Frankfort, Michigan, were caught by surprise. Winds up to 50-miles-per-hour swamped nearly 150 small boats. Some occupants of those boats didn't make it to shore. The reward for their disregard of storm warnings was death by drowning.

Lake Michigan is a huge body of water. Sudden winds turn its normally tranquil waters into surging masses of storm-tossed violence. When you consider coho fishing, make boat safety your most serious consideration. Lack of respect for the ferocious potential of Lake Michigan could cost you your life. Don't attempt this fishing without a seaworthy boat and dependable power. Observe all safety precautions with regard to boat equipment. Check advance weather reports, and keep an eye on developing weather conditions.

I've gone after cohos many times in a deep-hull 16-foot outboard powered with an 18-h.p. motor. We carry along a 10-h.p. motor for a

Safe fishing on the vast expanses of Lake Michigan calls for seaworthy boats. Though this scene shows calm water, sudden storms can create high seas in minutes.

spare in case of engine trouble. I consider this rig the minimum for coho fishing on the Great Lakes, and I wouldn't think of using it unless the fish were quite close to shore. In early spring and fall cohos can be caught from very close to shore to not more than 2 miles out. That can be safe 16-foot-boat territory on nice days. If the fish are farther out or bad weather is brewing, I wouldn't even think of using a 16-foot rig.

This is why coho fishing can be very expensive. If you want to cash in on the best and most fishing on your own you'll have to invest in a boat large enough to handle Lake Michigan during average weather conditions. Twenty- to 24-foot boats seem to be the vogue today. The expense factor is why the average guy who fishes for cohos only a few days a year goes the charter-boat route. For $20 to $30 per day, per person, you'll get an experienced captain, fully equipped boat with the latest electronic fish-finding gear, ship-to-shore radio and the best fishing equipment.

Charter-boat guide gaffs a typical coho for client. Charter operations are common at most port cities and towns along the Lake Michigan shoreline.

Small boats in the 16-foot class are okay on calm days when the action is found close to shore, but they're too dangerous when Lake Michigan gets rough.

Where and when to go after cohos is now pretty well defined. The year's action begins in April on the southern part of Lake Michigan. This may be the sportiest fishing because the cohos are now feeding near the surface and they'll recklessly hit most any trolled lure that flashes, wiggles or wobbles. This easy and productive fishing lasts into June when the schools begin migrating north.

The only drawback of the early fishing—if you consider it a drawback —is that the spring cohos run in the 3- to 5-pound class. You don't get the lunkers weighing up to 10 pounds and more till the fish have matured and schooled for spawning in late summer and early fall. By this time they're in the northern part of the lake. On the plus side, these smaller salmon are fighting fools, there are lots of them, and they strike with abandon.

Getting in on the spring action is no problem at all. Almost any port town or city from Kenosha, Wisconsin, to South Haven, Michigan, will be the base of coho addicts in April and May. Most ports have charter operations. Chambers of commerce in these cities recognize salmon fishing as a financial bonanza, and they go all out to help visiting anglers. A good bet is to write the chamber of commerce in several port cities and ask for advice as to when the fishing peaks. You can also ask for information on charter-boat operators, bait and tackle shops which cater to coho fishermen, and motel accommodations. It's best to make and finalize plans well in advance because the fishing area could be crowded. Southern Lake Michigan draws spring fishermen like a magnet because of its tremendous coho angling.

Early fall produces the next most dependable fishing. During mid-summer the salmon are migrating and they're also scattered all over the lake. It isn't till the spawning urge begins moving them toward their home streams where they were planted as fry that they begin schooling. As these schools increase in size and concentrate off river mouths, the great fall fishing hits its stride. Look for the action to begin about mid-August, hit its peak about Labor Day, and taper off into October.

Asking for information from chambers of commerce is a good bet for finding the fall action, too. On the Michigan side the top bases are Muskegon, Pentwater, Ludington, Manistee and Frankfort. In Wisconsin try any port city from Kenosha to Algoma. Timing your trip is more important in fall than in spring because coho schools begin forming first in the warmest water.

THE COHO STORY

Let's take the Michigan side as an example. The waters off Muskegon —in the southern part of the fall action range—will show peak fishing several weeks earlier than the waters off Manistee and Frankfort in the north. In contrast, when the action is fading in the south, it will be peaking in the north. This fact becomes all important for anglers who have to plan their trips during specific time periods.

The fall fishing produces slashing action with lunkers. If that's what you're after, by all means go in the fall. Fighting these bigger fish can turn your arms numb, even when you're using the relatively heavy trolling gear that has become standard for coho fishing.

Fall fishing for salmon in rivers and river mouths is just beginning to come on strong. If you want to catch a coho with lighter tackle than is used for trolling, if you don't like boat fishing, and if you want to rely more on skill than luck, then river or shoal fishing is for you.

Until recent years two assumptions held the shallow-water action in check. It was assumed that cohos stopped feeding as they moved into parent streams and that it was impossible to entice these fish into striking a lure. Second, it was common knowledge that salmon die after spawning. From this fact it was assumed that the fish had already deteriorated to the point where they weren't worth eating by the time they entered spawning streams.

It is now known that these assumptions are only partially true. Some cohos move into the rivers before they're ready to spawn. These fish are still silvery in color. Catch one of these and you'll have as fine an eating fish as any caught by trolling out on the lake. The darker-colored fish—those that are well along to spawning time—make excellent table fare when smoked. Lovers of smoked fish claim the river cohos are just as good eating as the lake salmon.

The myth that cohos wouldn't strike a lure after they moved into river mouths was exploded when a few exploratory anglers discovered the fish would hit small spoons and streamer flies. The river fish probably strike more out of anger and curiosity than hunger, but many will hit.

The shoal- and river-fishing boom is also coming on ever stronger because more and more coho fry are being planted in more rivers and streams. When the stocking program began back in the late 1960's only the major rivers were planted. In recent years cohos have been stocked in many small streams which offer great wading opportunities and fine

Not all coho fishing is limited to trolling from boats. This angler lands his prize near the mouth of Michigan's Platte River.

Catching cohos in rivers flowing to Lake Michigan is coming on strong.

shoal-fishing conditions near their mouths. Many of these streams go unnoticed by the crowds, but the fry planted in them return as unerringly to their parent currents as do the fry planted in larger rivers. Fisheries biologists claim that most of the salmon utilizing these smaller waters never see a lure.

So the unbelievable coho bonanza continues to roll. A decade ago there wasn't a single salmon in Lake Michigan. Today fishing for cohos is a billion-dollar industry. The action stretches from such unlikely places as the Chicago lakefront to little-known streams in Michigan's Upper Peninsula. The bonanza seems destined to continue rolling on far into the future.

There are party boats sailing from practically every port along the coast. These boats are fishing out of Captree State Basin on Long Island. They catch winter flounder during the cold weather months and summer flounder during the warm weather. If you don't have your own equipment, you may rent tackle aboard the packets.

The Lure
of Inshore Atlantic

MILT ROSKO

Stretching from the thin barrier islands of the Carolinas to the outermost tip of dune-covered Cape Cod as it juts into the Atlantic are some of the most heavily fished coastal waters in the Americas. People from all walks of life living in Boston, New York, Newark, Philadelphia, Wilmington, Baltimore, Washington and Norfolk, as well as the suburbs, turn to these waters during their leisure hours to test their skills with a wide variety of gamefish and bottom feeders.

During recent years the fishing that at one time was limited to the spring, summer and fall seasons has now expanded to the winter as well, with sportsmen enjoying the opportunity to wet a line both day and night.

Inshore fishing along the middle and north Atlantic coast falls into several distinct categories: party boat fishing, inshore bay and river fishing from small boats, bank, pier, bridge and bulkhead fishing, along with the challenge of fishing from the surf, jetties and breakwaters that stretch along the coast.

PARTY BOAT FISHING

I doubt if there's a bay, river, or harbor along the middle and north Atlantic coast where a party boat doesn't leave each day. Party boats, also called head boats and ground-fishing boats in some sectors, are big craft capable of fishing from 10 to upward of 75 or more anglers. The packets sail on a regular schedule, usually departing dockside anywhere from 5 to 8 A.M. every day, and returning to dockside around 4 P.M., giving the angler a long fishing day. Half-day boats usually leave later in the morning and return to dockside in mid-afternoon. There are also boats that sail on a night schedule, and these usually depart dockside at around 7 P.M., affording anglers an opportunity to enjoy some fishing after work. The boats return to the dock at midnight or a little later.

The best part about party boat fishing is that it's on a first-come first-serve basis with no reservation required. There is a basic fare for each type of fishing, which includes bait and chum. If you wish, you may rent tackle. Many of the larger packets have a galley on board, with soup, sandwiches, and hot and cold drinks available.

The mainstay of the party boat fleet is the bottom feeder. During the summer months, the tautog, porgy, sea bass, summer flounder, weakfish, spot, and croaker provide the bill of fare. In spring and fall it's Atlantic mackerel and winter flounders that give you fast action, while the winter months produce pollock, codfish, silver hake, and red hake.

Most of these bottom feeders aren't too difficult to catch. When the huge schools move inshore from the edge of the Continental Shelf the action can be fast and furious. I like to use a medium-weight party boat outfit. I find it serves me well throughout the year. The tip is light enough to enjoy tussling with a 1-pound flounder, yet there's enough backbone to coax a stubborn 25-pound codfish to gaff. The reel I use is a standard multiplying spool saltwater model capable of holding approximately 200 yards of 30-pound-test monofilament line. I always use a multiplying reel, as spinning tackle is designed for casting, and seldom is it practical to cast from a party boat.

The most popular terminal rig for bottom feeders is a high-low rig. The rig is designed to present one hook directly on the bottom, which is the low hook, and a second, or high hook, approximately 2 feet from

June Rosko landed this fine tautog, popularly called blackfish, while bottom fishing from a party boat off Cape May, N.J. The tautog is plentiful along the entire inshore middle Atlantic coast, and prefers rocky bottom, or areas around wrecks.

Here's the Peconic Queen returning to her berth at Montauk with a fine haul of codfish made from nearby waters. Often it's possible to land a dozen fine codfish in a single day's fast fishing. Most of the cod are caught while bottom fishing with sea clams as bait.

the bottom. This enables you to present a pair of baits on the floor of the bay, river, or open ocean.

Depth of water, wind velocity, and the swiftness of the current where you are fishing will determine the sinker weight you will require to hold bottom. Often a ½-ounce sinker is adequate when bay fishing in shallow water for winter flounders, while in the open reaches of the ocean where you have to send your baits to the bottom in 150 feet or more it may be necessary to use 12- to 16-ounce weights. It's important to have your sinker on the bottom, for seldom will these species venture more than a couple of feet off the bottom to take a bait. I make it a practice to use enough weight to keep my line perpendicular to the bottom, which gives me better control and enables me to feel the delicate strike of even a small bottom feeder.

The party boats usually supply clams, squid, or fillets of fresh fish as bait. It's important to use bait of a size most appropriate to the species you're after. If porgies or croakers are your target, a small No. 3 or 4 Claw-style hook is fine, and the bait you use should cover it, but not so large that a fish cannot easily inhale it. With summer flounders that range from 1 to 10 pounds or more you should use a 2/0 or 3/0 Carlisle if the fish are running consistently small, and move up to a 5/0 or 6/0 hook if there are a lot of 4- to 10-pounders being landed. Strips of squid, sand lance, spearing minnows and strips of fillets are all good baits for the summer flatties.

Codfish and pollock have a sizable mouth, and you'll find a 5/0 or 6/0 hook isn't too big. If there are heavyweights consistently being taken, you'll find a 7/0 or 8/0 Claw-style hook best. Clams are the preferred bait, but don't make the mistake of using such a large bait that a fish has difficulty getting it into its mouth.

Fiddler crabs are a favorite bait for tautog, called blackfish in some areas, and it's important to match the bait to the size of the hook and the general size of the fish being taken. Tautog have a small mouth and take the bait extremely fast, making a small, strong hook a must, with a No. 1 or 2 favored by most anglers.

While bottom fishing is without question the most popular technique employed by party boat anglers, chumming is also extremely popular, especially when species such as Atlantic mackerel, bluefish, school bluefin tuna, bonito and weakfish are schooled in an area.

Chumming consists of dropping pieces of food into the sea from an anchored or drifting boat. This chum drifts along with the current, and as fish begin to pick up pieces of the free-drifting food they follow it to its source, where they also find your baited hook drifting along with the chum.

The first species to respond to chum early in the spring is Atlantic mackerel. After wintering off the Virginia Capes, the mackerel begin their long trek north to spend the summer off New England and the Maritime Provinces. They're hungry and will readily move in to a chum line of finely ground menhaden. Menhaden, by the way, are called by a variety of names, including mossbunker or just plain bunker. They're an oily forage fish that make an excellent chum for most any species.

When the mackerel swarm into the chum line you can often see them by the thousands around the boat. At such times they'll quickly take a tiny piece of fresh fish on a No. 3 or 4 hook.

Rather than employ bait, some anglers use a jig and teaser combination. They tie a Diamond, Vike, or Hopkins No-Eql jig to the end of their line, and tie in via dropper loops two or three Norwegian tube teasers at intervals of about 1 foot ahead of the jig. The jig and teaser combo is drifted into the chum line and jigged vigorously, and it's not unusual to catch several mackerel at one time. Indeed, sometimes the fishing is so fast and furious that the boats head back to port after just a couple of hours with full fish bags.

But bluefish are the species that really generate enthusiasm among the chumming fraternity when they arrive. This is party boat sportfishing at its finest, with fish ranging from 3 to 18 pounds and more testing an angler's skill.

Terminal rigging when chumming for bluefish is minimal. Most anglers tie a small black barrel swivel directly to the end of their line, and then twist on a 6- to 8-inch leader of No. 8 or 9 stainless steel leader material, and finally their hook. If the fish are running small, say up to 5 pounds, a 4/0 or 5/0 hook is fine, but with the jumbo blues many anglers will use either a 6/0 or 7/0 size, with a Claw or Beak style preferred.

Bait is either a chunk of fresh butterfish or a piece cut from the back of a menhaden, although mackerel and herring chunks are often employed too. The hook should be placed well within the bait, but I usually leave the point and barb exposed, so that it may quickly penetrate once a fish takes it into its mouth.

A small rubber-cored sinker may be attached to the line if there is a

Here's Milt Rosko with a fine bluefish he landed while chumming from a party boat. Party boats sail both day and night during the height of the bluefish run, and it's not unusual to hook many of these fine fighters in a single trip. Chunks of butterfish and pieces of menhaden are the preferred bait.

swift current, as this takes the bait into the depths along with the chum. If current is slow and the bait tends to sink too quickly, then a small plastic or cork float is used to hold the bait at an intermediate level.

The key to chumming is always permitting the bait to drift naturally in the current. Once you've permitted it to drift out 100 feet or more, just reel it back in and begin over again. Don't lock your reel in gear and permit the bait to hang in the current, as it will invariably spin in an unnatural manner and not draw the strikes that a free-drifting bait will produce.

Often, during the late summer and especially in the fall, other species will invade the chum line intended for bluefish and a gamefishing bonanza will occur. Little tuna, school bluefin tuna, Atlantic bonito and oceanic bonito swarm into the chum line, and readily take a bait, providing anglers with mixed bags.

SMALL BOAT FISHING

Many anglers who begin fishing aboard the party packets develop such an enthusiasm for boat fishing that they soon join the contingent who purchase their own boats, or who charter a boat, or rent a small boat and outboard motor at one of the hundreds of boat rental liveries along the coast.

With your own boat or a rental you're your own skipper and can devote your time to the type of fishing you enjoy most. There's also the opportunity of using lighter tackle than is practical aboard the party packets, which makes for more fun.

It would be repetitious to cover the basic techniques employed for bottom fishing and chumming, as small boat anglers use essentially the same techniques and catch the same species as those who fish from the party boats.

There are several fine opportunities which are open to the small boat angler that are not available to party boat fishermen, specifically trolling, casting, and live-bait fishing. These techniques are most often employed by anglers who seek striped bass, bluefish, channel bass, and weakfish.

Trolling consists of systematically moving along slowly through known haunts of gamefish, with lures streaming behind the boat, with the speed of the boat regulated to impart action to the lures.

For the species mentioned earlier, trollers employ a wide variety of lures. Plugs are a favorite, with the surface and sub-surface swimmers, and popping plugs being the most popular. Spoons also bring many strikes, and trollers will use those measuring 3 or 4 inches for weakfish on up to 12-inch long and 4-inch wide bunker spoons for striped bass.

Bucktail jigs are another fine lure, and trollers most often use those ranging in weight from ½ through 4 ounces. Jigs account for all of these species, especially when they're feeding on small baitfish such as spearing and sand launce. The newer plastic-tailed jigs have also proved popular, especially with anglers after weakfish. Rigged eels account for a good share of strikes from stripers. Plastic tube lures in their many shapes, sizes, and colors bring many strikes from all major species sought by inshore trollers.

Up at Cape Cod you'll find that many anglers travel along the beach in beach buggies, and then launch small aluminum boats from the surf. They do extremely well with striped bass and bluefish during the summer.

The name "metal squid" covers a multitude of lure types, including such modern lures as the Hopkins and Kastmaster, along with the old original metal squid, usually made of block tin. These are all basically designed to imitate a small baitfish and are dressed with a feather or bucktail skirt, or with a piece of pork rind, all of which add to the appeal of the basic lure.

I use a medium-weight trolling rod when after stripers, blues, and channel bass, which measures 6½ feet in length and has a tip that provides maximum action with fish that frequently weigh 40 pounds or more. A 2/0 or 3/0 multiplying trolling reel capable of holding 200 yards of 30-pound-test monofilament works fine.

In rigging up terminal tackle for trolling, I use several feet of double line, with a spider knot, and then an offshore swivel knot to attach a Sampo ball-bearing swivel and coastlock snap. Next I use a 6- to 8-foot length of 50-pound-test nylon leader material, at the end of which is a duo-lock snap to which I attach my lure.

Vin T. Sparano with two big striped bass, 41- and 44-pounders, taken by trolling big plugs from a small boat off Montauk, New York.

You'll find plenty of rowboat liveries along the middle and north Atlantic, where for a nominal rental fee you can enjoy the use of a boat and motor for inshore fishing. The scene here is at Cerullo Brothers on Moriches Bay in Long Island.

Occasionally, when I want to get my lures deep, I use a torpedo-shaped trolling sinker between the coastlock snap and leader. The sinkers may range from 1 to 5 ounces, and are particularly effective when you're fishing in water of moderate depth. When I want to get down near the bottom in 25 or 30 feet of water, it would require just too much sinker weight, so then I employ wire line, usually solid Monel, which helps get the lures down very deep to where the fish are feeding.

Unlike the tuna and bonito, which are not shy and frequently swarm into the wake of a boat to strike lures trolled on short lines, striped bass, bluefish, channel bass and weakfish require a longer line behind the boat. The shortest line I usually troll is approximately 100 feet and more often than not I've 125 feet trailing astern.

The key in trolling is to fish a pattern so that all the lures are working properly behind the boat, which is accomplished by having the right combination of speed and current. Too fast or too slow results in the lures hanging listlessly, or spinning, all to no avail.

Once the lures are working properly, troll through known haunts of the gamefish you are seeking. This may be along the edge of a channel where the water drops off abruptly, or where there is broken, irregular rocky bottom where fish congregate to feed. Look for strikes where a tide rip forms, for frequently baitfish will collect there and the bass, blues and weaks know it will be easy pickings.

Of course, there are times when fish will move out into the open reaches of a bay or the ocean to feed, and then it's simply a matter of covering a lot of water and searching them out. Always keep alert for schools of baitfish on the surface, and take special notice of sea gulls wheeling and diving over baitfish, for this usually denotes hungry game-fish feeding beneath the surface. Never move right through the school, but instead work the perimeter, making lazy circles so that your lures skirt the edge, and you'll be rewarded with strikes.

The beauty part of trolling is that you can continually move to new areas, probing with your lures as you go, until you hit a concentration of fish.

Small-boat anglers sometimes tire of trolling, and they may switch to casting tackle. Casting is especially effective when fish are feeding on the surface, or when they're feeding in spots that do not lend themselves well to trolling, such as around rocky promontories or along the surf and where breakers crash on outer bars along the beach. Casting enables you to use lighter tackle than is generally the case with trolling.

Either multiplying or spinning tackle may be employed while casting from a small boat. I alternate between both outfits, using rods that measure approximately 7 feet in overall length. I use 20-pound-test line with the conventional outfit, and 15-pound-test monofilament line with the spinning reel, with both reels loaded with approximately 200 yards of line, which I've found to be more than adequate for inshore gamefish.

Casters use three basic lures: bucktail jigs, plugs, and metal squids, with a fourth choice rigged eels for striped bass devotees. All of these lure types lend themselves well to casting, with weights ranging ½ to 3 ounces being the most popular, as they are easily handled with medium-weight casting tackle.

You've got to know your water, for otherwise you might find yourself spending hours fruitlessly casting to spots where fish simply don't congregate. A good rule of thumb is to fish spots where you know fish are taken regularly and where there always seems to be an abundance of natural bait. Look for jetty fronts and breakwaters to be spots where bait seeks sanctuary, and you'll find gamefish close behind. Tide rips are always good, as are tidal flats that drop off into deep water. The mouths of creeks and rivers, where they empty into a bay or ocean are still other spots where gamefish will come to feed.

Remember that when casting it's up to you to impart action to your lure. With bucktail jigs the most effective technique is to permit them to settle into the depths and then retrieve with a whip-retrieve, causing the lure to dart ahead and then falter, much like a wounded baitfish, which usually tempts gamefish into striking. With plugs you've got to vary your retrieve. Some plugs, like the surface swimmers, work best when retrieved very slowly, while with popping plugs a sweeping movement of the rod tip causes the plug to pop and gurgle as you retrieve it, which excites strikes from hungry gamesters. If you don't get strikes immediately, try varying your speed of retrieve. Sometimes that's all it takes to bring strikes.

Some of the most exciting channel-bass fishing I've ever experienced was off Virginia's Barrier Islands. We would cruise in a small boat on a sunny spring day and watch for schools of big channel bass cruising just beneath the surface. Maintaining respectable distance so as not to spook the school, we would then cast a Hopkins lure into the school of traveling fish. It proved great sport, with most of the fish averaging from 35 to 45 pounds.

In recent years inshore small boat anglers have taken to fishing with live baits in earnest, and have accounted for many fine catches of striped bass and bluefish. Their shore-based brethren who fish from the beach and jetties also account for many fine catches, particularly of large fish.

It isn't difficult fishing live bait, but the problem often comes with obtaining the live bait. Baits such as live menhaden, mackerel, herring and eels are the favorites, and are either netted or fished for individually, and then used for bait.

Terminal rigging with these baits is easy. Many anglers simply tie a 7/0 or 8/0 Claw-style hook directly to the end of their line, slip the hook into the baitfish's lips and permit it to stream out into the current. Some anglers prefer to use a treble hook instead of a single hook, and they use either a 3/0 or 4/0 treble with fine results, using just one of the three hooks to secure the bait, with the remaining hooks in position to penetrate once a fish takes the bait.

Sometimes a small sinker is added to the line to help take the bait deep, but the key is permitting it to swim as freely and as naturally as possible. While the majority of anglers hook their baits through the lips, there is much to be said for hooking the bait lightly just ahead of the dorsal fin. I suspect it's like everything else in saltwater fishing, just a matter of what you get used to.

The salt water killie, popularly called minnow, is a very popular bait for summer flounders. Drifted along the bottom, or slowly trolled, it readily brings strikes from the summer flatties.

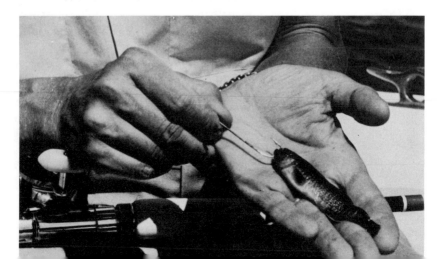

Milt Rosko just netted this fine tiderunner weakfish for his daughter, Linda, who hooked the beauty while drifting a sandworm bait on the bottom. Fish of this size are quite plentiful in inshore waters and provide fine sport on a light outfit.

While not large, winter flounder are one of the first species to put in an appearance in the spring. On a good day it's often possible to catch several dozen of the tasty bottom feeders. A chum pot of ground fish helps attract the flatties to your sandworm or bloodworm baits.

The key to fishing with live baits, and many of these baits measure from 8 to 14 inches, with eels going even longer, is giving a big striped bass or bluefish, or even a tiderunner weakfish, ample time to take the bait and get it well into its mouth.

I always keep my reel in free spool, or, if using spinning tackle, I keep the bail open. When a fish picks up the bait I let it take line freely. Sometimes a fish will move off with 25 to 50 feet of line, and I still hesitate. I've found that by waiting until the fish appears to begin swimming at a rapid speed before striking I hook more fish than when they first take the bait and appear to be toying with it. On the average, I think you'll hook far more fish by hesitating and letting the fish take 50 feet or more of line, than you will by striking too soon.

Early in the season, before the huge schools of forage species make an appearance on the inshore grounds, many stripers and weakfish may be taken while bottom fishing with natural baits such as crabs, sea-worms and clams. This is easy fishing, and may be done from a drifting or anchored boat, or while casting from a breakwater, pier or the surf. The preferred rig is made by tying a three-way swivel directly to the end of your line, then tying a sinker in via a 6- or 8-inch dropper loop, and tying a 30-inch leader to the remaining eye of the swivel. To the end of the leader, tie a No. 1 or 1/0 Claw- or Beak-style hook when using bloodworms and sandworms as bait, and a 2/0 to 4/0 size when crabs and clams are used.

Fishing with natural baits is a waiting game and requires a great deal of patience. But once you hit a spot where a lot of fish are feeding, the rewards can be great, for you can take fish after fish from the same spot as they move along the bottom searching for a meal.

Bob Rosko unhooks a fine summer flounder for Joe Basilio while fishing at Sandy Hook, New Jersey. The flatties are a bottom feeder and will take a variety of baits, including live minnows, spearing, sand eels, strips of squid and especially strips of fluke belly. Drifting or slow trolling produces best results.

Surfmen must have patience. But their wait often pays off with gamefish such as striped bass, bluefish, weakfish and channel bass.

SURF AND JETTY FISHING

I've left until last what I feel to be one of the most rewarding types of inshore fishing there is along the middle Atlantic and north Atlantic coasts. Fishing from the surf and the many rock jetties and natural rock promontories that extend seaward along our coast holds challenges galore and provide experienced anglers with phenomenal sport throughout the season.

Small channel bass are plentiful along the Carolina surf. They feed very close to shore and will take a small piece of mullet bait fished just beyond the breakers. When after small species many surfmen use a two-hook rig.

The species that frequent the surf at one time or another are legion, and include practically every species I've mentioned thus far. Summer and winter flounders are regularly taken from the beaches, as are tautog, weakfish, mackerel, and occasionally porgies and sea bass. Striped bass and bluefish are regular visitors, and in New England it's not uncommon to catch pollock and codfish right from the sand beaches during cold weather. Channel bass are landed regularly by beach-based anglers, and each season sees many 40- to 50-pounders landed by skillful anglers.

So you see, if boat fishing isn't your forte, there's plenty of action

Bob Rosko hooked this fine striper while casting a rigged eel from a coastal jetty. Night fishing from the jetties produces best results, as the stripers usually are more active after sundown. Jetty jockies also take many bluefish and weakfish, with plugs and bucktail jigs producing many strikes.

awaiting you on the sand and rockpiles. With bottom feeders, the techniques employed are much the same as we explained earlier for boat fishing. It's a matter of matching hook size and bait to the size of the species in residence and having the patience to sit and wait for strikes. Sometimes bottom fishing with natural baits will be extremely productive. Indeed, I've frequently employed either crabs, chunks of mackerel or spot as bait when it proved to be the only way I could score with such gamefish as striped bass, channel bass, weakfish and bluefish. And I don't mean small fish either, as some of the heaviest of these species I've ever landed were taken on natural baits.

But perhaps the most exciting sport of all is to seek stripers, blues and weaks with artificials from the sand and rockpiles. For this type of fishing I generally employ a stiff-action rod that measures anywhere from 7 to 8 feet in overall length. I shy away from the extremely long surf rods, as I don't find I need a long rod. The extra-long rod is overpowering, which results in it being a handicap rather than an advantage to use.

I tend to use reels smaller than most anglers, for I find a spinning or conventional reel capable of holding 200 yards of line is more than adequate. In my mind, when a striper takes 200 yards of line he deserves to get away! I simply have not yet encountered a situation where I required a reel holding 400 yards of line, yet I regularly observe anglers using these overpowering winches on beaches and rockpiles.

Because I'm fishing from spots where rocks and sand frequently come in contact with the line, I generally use 17-pound-test monofilament. The line is a bit heavier than the 12- and 15-pound line used by many surfmen, but I find it's good insurance, especially when I hook a striper in the 30- or 40-pound class and I have to put a lot of pressure on it to get it to the rocks or through the crashing breakers.

The arsenal of lures available to the surfman is so extensive that I suspect it is often the downfall of many individuals who simply buy every lure imaginable, and try to use them all. As a result they fail to build confidence in any one lure, and they fail to score regularly, simply because they're trying too many lures.

For my rockpile and beach endeavors I select a few basic lure types that have given me consistent results over the years and I stick with them. The rigged eel, measuring approximately 12 to 14 inches, is always in my surf bag from May until December, as they're one of the finest striper producers there is. I also carry several bucktail jigs, with ½- to 1½-ounce models for surf and jetty work, and models up to 3 ounces when I fish beachways and inlets.

For daytime work, I include popping plugs. But given a choice of plugs, I would stick with a surface swimmer with calm water conditions and a sub-surface swimmer when the surf is rough, especially at night. I also include deep-running Mirrolure plugs in my kit when there's a sea running, as I find these get deeper faster than most other plug types. For rough water I'll include a few old-time block tin squids in my sack, weighing about 1½ to 2 ounces, which I dress with a piece of pork rind. For really reaching out when fish are well off the beach I find the Hopkins difficult to beat. It's made of stainless steel and casts like a bullet.

I don't usually carry all of these lures with me at one time. After a while you get the feel as to which lures to carry. If there's a heavy sea running and strong wind it's foolish to take a ½-ounce plug or tiny bucktail jigs onto the beach or jetty. You get the feel, and simply carry enough lures so that you're not overburdened and are sufficiently mobile to move from spot to spot with ease. Everything I take with me is either in my pockets or a canvas surf shoulder bag, and a light one at that.

I use a spider knot and double the last 2 feet of my terminal end of the line, and then use either an offshore swivel knot or an improved clinch knot to tie a barrel swivel to the line. Next comes about 24 inches of 30-pound-test nylon leader material, and a small duo-lock snap. So rigged, I'm ready to snap on a rigged eel, bucktail jig, or plug and go fishing.

With the passage of years the sea has eroded much of our coastline, and as a result the federal and state governments have built breakwaters and jetties to hold back the ravages of the ocean. In many areas this has eliminated the bar formations usually found along beaches, and caused many sections of beach to sand in. As a result, where the jetties are plentiful many anglers now ply their sport from the rockpiles as they find the fish move around the rocks looking for food. Better fishing is often experienced from the rocks than from the adjacent beaches.

When fishing from a rockpile I always wear either boots or waders with golf soles attached to the soles, which secures my footing on the slippery moss-covered rocks. You can also use ice creepers, which may be secured to your boots via canvas straps, and they're quite serviceable, but not as comfortable as the golf soles or golf rubbers. I also wear a foul-weather suit to keep dry in case there's a lot of spray, which is usually the case. A miner's headlamp around my neck is a must when night fishing. I always carry a gaff, either a short one when the surf is calm, or a 6-foot jetty gaff when it's rough.

As I move onto a rockpile I try to judge where the fish are apt to be feeding. Sometimes they'll herd bait back in the pocket where the beach and rockpile meet. At other times they'll be searching around the rocks that are tumbled to the side of the jetty, or perhaps feeding in the rips that form along the jetty front as the current moves parallel with the beach and then around the front of the rocks.

I systematically work my lures through all of these spots, casting a moderate distance from the jetty and making certain I work the lure right to the edge of the rocks, for experience has taught me that many of my strikes come within a few feet of the rocks.

I've found that with rigged eels, a deep moderate retrieve works best. Here the key is making a cast, then hesitating until the eel gets a chance to settle to the bottom before you begin retrieving. This technique also works with bucktail jigs, metal squids, and deep-diving plugs. I suspect that more people retrieve their lures far above the heads of feeding gamefish than do those who keep the lure down where the fish are feeding. On the average, the deep retrieve always brings more strikes for me. Unless, of course, the fish can be observed feeding on top, and even then, sometimes, the deep retrieve brings more strikes.

I always like to move around a lot when I'm climbing around rock-piles. I select those to fish which are usually devoid of anglers, for I find I can catch more fish if I have the spot to myself. I can also move around more freely and fish the spot the way I want to, not hampered by others.

Tides play an important role in selecting the spots you plan to fish along the surf and jetties. A deeply cut beach may produce great results at either low or high tide, but a shallow beach with an offshore bar formation may not have enough water to even hold any fish at low tide. In the case of jetties, some are only accessible at low tide, and are covered on the flood. Other jetties have lots of water and produce good fishing at high tide, but have sand beach surrounding them at the bottom of the tide. This makes it important for you to study the beaches and rockpiles you plan to fish, and to take the tides into consideration in determining which spots you fish on a given day or night.

I should note that the finest surf and jetty fishing I've ever experienced has always been at night. It seems the fish move in to feed more readily during the hours of darkness, although I've also experienced good sport at dusk and daybreak.

There are many piers extending seaward into the ocean and many bays along the coast, and lots of anglers experience fine fishing from them. I've also enjoyed fine fishing from the bulkheads that line rivers and canals and caught many bottom feeders from the bridges that span these waterways and from which fishing is permitted. Bottom fishing usually produces best, but I've caught some school stripers, small blues and weakfish while working bucktail jigs from these structures, particularly during the evening hours.

One can readily appreciate that the angler who elects to do his fishing inshore along the middle Atlantic coast has a wide variety of fishing opportunities to satisfy his appetite. There's a type of fishing available to the newcomer and veteran angler, for the family man and his wife and youngsters. There's easy fishing for bottom feeders that are eager to cooperate, and there's demanding sport from tough gamefish that will call on every bit of skill you can muster. It's all here. Take your pick and you're certain to enjoy many pleasant fishing adventures along this long stretch of the majestic Atlantic.

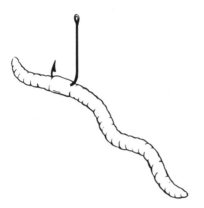

Worm hooked through collar or girdle is best for stream fishing. The worm is allowed to drift naturally in current.

Good way to thread a worm for stillfishing for panfish.

Two ways to hook a live minnow. Top, run hook just behind dorsal fin if you're stillfishing. Bait will swim naturally. Below, run hook up through lips if you're trolling and fishing from drifting boat.

The Natural Baits
In Fresh and Salt Water

VIN T. SPARANO

Live bait is the real thing! Even the most avid purist would concede that live bait, when properly presented, is one of the deadliest of all lures. Many times, however, live bait is incorrectly rammed on a hook and chunked into the water. When this happens, the bait does not act naturally, may die quickly, and will likely turn away lunkers that grew big by learning how to recognize food that "doesn't look right."

Live bait will only appear natural if placed on the hook correctly, and placing a bait on a hook correctly depends on how you plan to fish it. You wouldn't, for example, hook a minnow behind the dorsal fin if you plan on trolling. Minnows just don't swim backwards. Let's take a look at the popular baits and learn how to hook them.

Even though common garden worms and nightcrawlers will take most species of fish, they must still be presented differently. Worms are not native to water. They find their way into streams and lakes during rains when they are washed into the water. They must be presented accordingly. A worm washed into a stream, for example, would drift with the current, so it should also be fished that way. Hook it once through the collar or girdle with both ends free to drift naturally, fish it with no line drag, and let the current do the work. The worm should look strung out, bouncing along quickly through riffles and slowly through pools.

Using worms for panfish requires a different tact. Generally, the panfisherman is stillfishing, so natural presentation is less important. A single worm should be used and threaded about three times on the hook. If you're still bothered by nibblers, use only a piece of worm and thread it on the hook, covering the point and barb completely. Nightcrawlers are effective on big bass, and many fishermen stillfish for bass with the big worms the same way they would for panfish. Actually, bass prefer a moving bait and anglers would catch more lunkers if they cast and retrieved nightcrawlers slowly along the bottom. Hook the worm by running the point of the hook into the worm's head, bringing the point and barb out 1 inch below the head. Rigged this way and retrieved slowly, a nightcrawler will appear to be crawling on the bottom.

For such bottom feeders as catfish and suckers, natural presentation is not too important. Two or three worms threaded several times on a hook is sufficient. Simply let the gob of worms rest on the bottom. Big catfish will ordinarily just suck in the whole bait.

Next on the list of the most common live baits are the minnows, from 1-inchers for panfish to 8-inchers for big fish. There are two ways of hooking a live minnow and how an angler intends to fish determines which one to use. When trolling or fishing from a drifting boat, run the hook upward and through both lips of the minnow. The lip-hooked bait will move through the water on an even keel and look natural.

If you're stillfishing from an anchored boat or shoreline, hook the minnow just behind dorsal fin. Be careful not to run the hook too deep or it will hit the spine and kill the bait. Hooked just behind the fin, a minnow can swim freely and for a surprisingly long time. There is no hook weight near its head or tail to throw it off balance.

Frogs rank as another excellent bait for bass, pike, walleyes, and similar species. Stick with the small frogs, however, such as the leopard and green frogs. They are easy to find along any shoreline or riverbank during summer. There is really only one good way to hook a live frog and that is under the jaw and up through both lips. Cast it out and let the frog swim freely, or use a twitch-and-pause retrieve. A lip-hooked frog will stay alive for a long time.

A frog can also be hooked through one of its hind legs. A hook

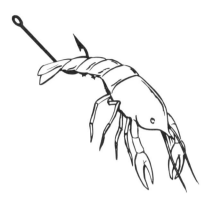

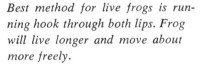

Best method for live frogs is running hook through both lips. Frog will live longer and move about more freely.

Only one good way to hook a crayfish so that it will stay alive and active for a reasonable length of time, and that's running hook up and through the tail.

through a frog's leg, however, will destroy some leg muscles, limiting its natural movements and taking away the natural look.

The crayfish or crawfish is another top bait for bass and trout. The best way to hook a crayfish is to run the hook up, through, and out the top of its tail. Cast into rocky shorelines or streams; they'll account for big trout and bass.

Salamanders or newts also take bass, trout, and similar species. Finding salamanders isn't hard. They like small springs and streams. They're active at night and easily spotted with a flashlight. Salamanders are fragile and must be hooked carefully. Use a thin-wire hook and run it through the lips or the tail. Salamanders produce best when drifted along streams and river bottoms.

We've covered the popular live baits, but there are still others worth mentioning. The hellgrammite, for example, ranks high with bass and trout. A water insect, hellgrammites average 1 to 2 inches and can be caught in most streams by simply turning over rocks and holding a net just downstream from the rock. The hellgrammite has a hard collar just behind the head and this is where the hook should be run through.

109

Nymphs, an underwater stage of an aquatic fly, is still another top bait, particularly for trout. Nymphs differ in the way they behave. Some crawl on rocks, others climb shoreline growths, and still others float downstream. They will all eventually hatch into flies, but it is during this nymphal period that they can be effectively used for bait. There are two ways to put nymphs on a hook. They can be completely threaded, running the hook from the rear, through the body, and up to the head. Or they can be simply hooked once just behind the head.

Grasshoppers also work well and finding them is no problem. Most grassy fields are loaded with 'hoppers. Use a butterfly net and you can fill a box quickly. It's easier to catch them at dawn and dusk. During midday, they are most active and spooky. There are several varieties of grasshoppers and nearly all take fish. There are grasshopper harnesses available, but I have found that they are more trouble than they're worth. It's best to use a thin-wire hook, running it down and through, behind the head.

The saltwater fisherman's choice of live bait may not be as broad as the freshwater man, but he nevertheless has the problem of learning how to get live bait on the hook so that it will look natural. Five of the most basic live baits for salt water are the shrimp, the blood- and sand-worm, the eel, and the various crabs.

The shrimp, which will catch most species, are hooked in pretty much the same manner as the freshwater crayfish. Run the hook upward, through, and out the top of the tail.

The bloodworm and the sandworm are to salt water what the night-crawler is to fresh water.

The sandworm will just about draw any inshore fish that spots it. Many anglers, however, make the mistake of threading these worms several times on a hook, so that they look like a mess rather than a live sandworm in a tidal flow. The correct way to hook a sandworm is once through the head, bringing the barb out about 1 inch or so from the head.

Hooking a bloodworm varies only slightly. Bloodworms tend to lose "body" after a few casts and appear stringy. When this happens, it's probably wise to put two or three bloodworms, depending on size, on the hook. The only time this method varies is when fishing for small fish, such as winter flounder. Because such species have small mouths

110

Salamanders or newts are fragile and should be hooked carefully with fine wire hooks. Least damaging way to rig this bait is hooking it through both lips (top). Salamanders can also be hooked through the tail, though this may restrict natural movement.

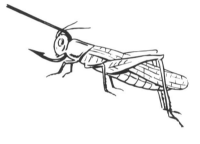

Hellgrammite should be hooked through collar just behind head.

Grasshoppers should be hooked just behind head with a thin-wire hook. Such a hook is necessary because grasshoppers are fragile.

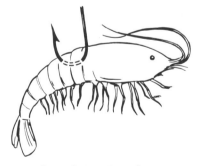

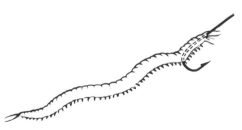

Hooking shrimp for salt-water fishing is pretty much the same as for crayfish in fresh water. Run hook through tail as shown.

Sandworm is hooked once through head so that barb is exposed an inch or so below head.

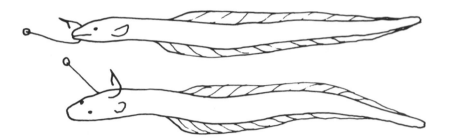

Eels will stay alive a long time if hooked through lips (top) or just beneath skin behind head (bottom).

Crabs are best hooked once through back section, as shown. Remove claws.

and huge numbers can be caught, it is advisable to cut these seaworms into small sections and place the small bits on your hook.

Live eels score high as striped bass and bluefish baits. An eel is at its best when allowed to swim freely. They can be hooked upward through both lips, or lightly through the skin behind the head. Take care not to run the hook too deep or you will hit the spine and kill the eel. Hooked properly, a live eel will literally last for hours until a big striper decides to make a meal of it.

Lastly are the various crabs, which will take species ranging from the small blackfish to big tarpon. There are several ways to hook a crab, but it has been my experience that once through the back section works

112

best. The point and barb of the hook should be exposed and it's also a good idea to break off the claws. Be careful when running the hook through the shell. Go too deep and you'll injure the crab and restrict its movement.

We've covered more than a few of the popular natural baits for both fresh and salt water, but by no means have we discussed all the various baits available to fishermen. Only by experience will you learn what works best in your waters. The accompanying natural-bait charts will give you a good start on learning what baits are effective and preferred for the various species of gamefish in fresh and salt water.

NATURAL BAITS FOR SALT WATER

Species	*Baits*
Amberjack	Strip baits
Barracuda	Bait fish
Bass, California kelp	Sardine, anchovy, clam, mussel, sea worm, shrimp
Bass, channel	Mullet, mossbunker, crab, clam
Bass, giant sea	Cut bait, mullet, mackerel, sardines
Bass, sea	Squid, clam, sea worm, crab, killie
Bass, striped	Sea worm, clam, eel, live mackerel, or mossbunker
Billfish (sailfish, marlin, swordfish)	Balao, mackerel, squid, bonito, strip baits
Bluefish	Rigged eel, cut bait, butterfish
Bonefish	Cut bait (mainly sardine and conch)
Codfish	Clam, crab, cut bait
Croaker	Sand bugs, mussel, clam, sardine, sea worm
Dolphin	Bait fish
Eel	Killie, clam, crab, sea worm, spearing
Flounder, summer	Squid, sparing, sea worm, clam, killie, smelt
Flounder, winter	Sea worm, mussel, clam

Species	Baits
Grouper	Squid, mullet, sardine, balao, shrimp, crab
Grunt	Shrimp, crab, sea worm
Haddock	Clam, conch, crab, cut bait
Hake	Clam, conch, crab, cut bait
Halibut	Squid, crab, sea worm, killie, shrimp
Jack Crevalle	Bait fish, cut bait
Jewfish	Mullet, other bait fish
Ladyfish	Killie, shrimp
Ling	Clam, crab, cut bait
Mackerel	Bait fish
Perch, white	Sea worm, shrimp, sparing
Pollack	Squid strip, clam
Pompano	Sand bugs
Porgy	Clam, squid, sea worm, crab, mussel, shrimp
Rockfish, Pacific	Herring, sardine, mussel, squid, clam, shrimp
Snapper, mangrove	Cut bait, shrimp
Snapper, red	Shrimp, mullet, crab
Snapper, yellowtail	Shrimp, mullet, crab
Snook	Crab, shrimp, bait fish
Sole	Clam, sea worm
Spot	Crab, shrimp, bait fish, sea worm
Tarpon	Cut bait, bait fish
Tautog (blackfish)	Clam, sea worm, crab, shrimp
Tomcod	Clam, mussel, shrimp
Tuna, bluefin	Mackerel, flying fish, bonito, squid, dolphin, herring, cut bait
Wahoo	Bait fish
Weakfish	Shrimp, squid, sea worm
Whiting, northern	Sea worm, clam
Yellowtail	Herring, sardine, smelt

THE NATURAL BAITS IN FRESH AND SALT WATER

Species	Baits
Bass, largemouth	Minnows, nightcrawlers, caterpillars, hellgrammites, grasshoppers, newts, salamanders, frogs, suckers, dragonflies, darters, sculpins, cut bait (perch belly, etc.), freshwater shrimp (scud)
Bass, smallmouth	Minnows, nightcrawlers, caterpillars, crayfish, hellgrammites, grasshoppers, newts, salamanders, frogs, suckers, freshwater shrimp (scud), dragonflies, darters, sculpins, cut bait (perch belly, etc.)
Trout	Minnows, earthworms, nightcrawlers, crickets, grubs, caterpillars, crayfish, hellgrammites, nymphs (mayfly, caddisfly, stonefly, and others), grasshoppers, newts, and salamanders, freshwater shrimp (scud), darters, salmon eggs
Pike	Minnows, nightcrawlers, frogs, suckers, cut bait (perch belly, etc.)
Walleyes	Minnows, nightcrawlers, crayfish, hellgrammites, newts, salamanders, frogs, darters, sculpins, cut bait (perch belly, etc.)
Pickerel	Minnows, nightcrawlers, newts, salamanders, frogs, darters, sculpins, cut bait (perch belly, etc.)
Muskellunge	Nightcrawlers, frogs, suckers, cut bait (perch belly, etc.)
Crappies	Minnows, earthworms, crickets, grubs, caterpillars, nymphs (mayfly, caddisfly, stonefly, and others), grasshoppers, wasp larvae, freshwater shrimp (scud), dragonflies, darters
Perch	Minnows, earthworms, crickets, grubs, caterpillars, nymphs (mayfly, caddisfly, stonefly, and others), grasshoppers, wasp larvae, freshwater shrimp (scud)
Sunfish	Earthworms, crickets, grubs, caterpillars, nymphs (mayfly, caddisfly, stonefly, and others), wasp larvae, freshwater shrimp (scud)

115

Species	Baits
Rock Bass	Minnows, earthworms, crickets, grubs, caterpillars, hellgrammites, newts, salamanders, wasp larvae, freshwater shrimp (scud), dragonflies, darters, sculpins
White Bass	Earthworms, dragonflies
Whitefish	Earthworms
Salmon, landlocked	Nymphs (mayfly, caddisfly, stonefly, and others)
Salmon	Salmon eggs
Sturgeon	Nightcrawlers
Catfish	Earthworms, nightcrawlers, crayfish, hellgrammites, newts, salamanders, doughballs
Carp	Doughballs

Anglers are often puzzled if they have to catch and keep something other than a dozen worms for a day's fishing. Catching the various natural baits and keeping them alive and kicking is not difficult. It can even be fun. The rewards are often better fishing and less money spent at bait shops.

Worms, whether earthworms or nightcrawlers, are the most popular live baits. Locating a source is rarely farther than your backyard, but there are a few tips that will make the job easier.

Nightcrawlers get their name from the fact that they come to the surface at night. They like warm and wet weather. Wait until it has been dark at least 2 to 3 hours, then prowl around your lawn, a golf course, or a park. Use a flashlight, but not one with a bright beam. This is one time weak batteries are an asset. If the beam is too bright, cover the lens with red cellophane. When you spot a worm, grab it by the head (the thicker end) with your fingers. If the worm tries to shoot back into the hole, hold onto one end until the worm releases tension and is free of the hole. You can also press your finger lightly against the worm's body where it enters its hole, cutting off the worm's escape.

If you can't find nightcrawlers at night, it's probably too dry for them to come to the surface. You can either wait for rain or water your lawn in the afternoon and go worm hunting that night. In summer, I sprinkle my lawn on Thursday and Friday, so I can collect enough worms for the weekend.

If you're after the common earthworm, which is smaller than the nightcrawler, you'll have to dig for them. Concentrate on compost heaps, vegetable gardens, and stream banks.

A day's supply of worms can be carried in a few inches of damp soil in a coffee can on which both ends have been removed. Punch holes in two of the plastic lids that come with the can. With two of these lids in place, it can be opened from either end for easy access to worms on the bottom. If you keep this container in a burlap pouch and dip it occasionally in a cool creek, the worms will stay fresh all day.

Commercial boxes for worms, as well as other baits, are available from Oberlin Bait Canteens. They are made of porous fiberboard, which insulates the box and keeps the inside cool and humid.

If you want to keep a good supply of worms on hand, build a worm

A day's supply of worms can easily be kept in a can of this size. Top and bottom of the can are removed and plastic lids (which come with the can) are used. Worms always crawl to the bottom, so this double lid makes worms at bottom easily accessible. Punch holes in the plastic lid and carry the can in burlap pouch. Every so often, dip the whole thing in water. The wet burlap will keep the worms cool and fresh.

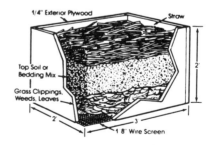

1/4" Exterior Plywood   Straw

Top Soil or
Bedding Mix

Grass Clippings,
Weeds, Leaves

2'

2'

3'

1 8' Wire Screen

Worm Box—Simple wood box with screen bottom can keep about 700 nightcrawlers on hand if sunk in soil in shady spot.

117

box. In a box (2x3x2 feet), you can house 600 or 700 nightcrawlers. Sink the box in a shady spot, allowing 2 inches of the box above ground. Damp and cool are the key words in keeping worms fresh. A wet burlap bag over the straw will work well. You might also try spreading out a few handfuls of ice cubes on the straw every two or three days. The ice will keep the soil damp and cool as it melts. Food is no problem, since worms eat most anything. I use coffee grounds, bread crumbs, and cornmeal.

Ice cubes, incidentally, can be effectively used when transporting and keeping worms on an extended fishing trip. Try the following method on your next trip. In the center of your bait box, which should measure about 12x12x8 inches deep if you're carrying 400 or so worms, clear a space in the bedding about 4 inches in diameter. Next, fill a glass jar or plastic container with ice cubes, screw the cap back on, and put it in a plastic bag sealed with a wire wrap. Place the container in the center of the box and push the bedding or soil around it.

The jar of ice will keep the soil cool and damp, and it will stay that way until the cubes melt. In hot weather, the worms will actually crowd around the jar. The purpose of the plastic bag is to seal in condensation. Without the plastic, the soil would become too soggy for worms.

Seaworms, such as blood and sandworms, are delicate and should be kept in damp seaweed. If they are to be kept for a week or so, spread them out in damp seaweed and keep them in a refrigerator at 40 degrees. Blood and sandworms are enemies and should not be kept together. I use a wood partition to divide my bait box into two compartments and it works okay. On surf fishing trips, I dip the entire box in the wash. The seaworms will stay in good shape for hours, even in direct sunlight.

Minnows rank second as the most popular bait and they can be caught almost as easily as worms. There are several ways to collect minnows: the minnow trap, the drop or umbrella net, or the minnow seine.

The minnow trap requires the least skill and it's a good one to use if you can set it close to home and check it regularly. It works on the principle that a small fish will swim into the funnellike openings after food and be unable to find its way out. For bait, wet oatmeal or cornmeal and roll it into balls the size of golfballs. The meal will break up gradually in the trap and provide bait for long periods.

Best place to set the trap is in shallow water near a dock or boat-

118

house. On streams, set it near the head or side of a pool where the current is slow.

The drop or umbrella net, which measures 3x3 feet, gets more immediate results but may be more difficult to use. Lower it into the water just deep enough so that you can still lift it fast. Sprinkle bread crumbs over it and let them sink. When minnows begin to feed on the crumbs, lift the net fast. With practice, you'll make good hauls every time.

Here's how I transport a lot of worms in an Oberlin Bait Canteen on lengthly fishing trips. The jar in the center of the bedding is full of ice cubes and sealed in a plastic bag. The plastic bag keeps condensation from getting into the bedding and making it too soggy. The ice will keep the worms cool and fresh. You'll even notice that worms will gather around the jar. If you're making a long car trip, I suggest dropping a few ice cubes on top of the bedding. They will provide additional cooling and moisture to the bedding as the ice melts.

Some baits cannot be kept together, such as blood and sand worms. These two sea worms are enemies and will injure one another. I solved the problem with a simple wood partition in my bait box. The same can be done with incompatible fresh-water baits.

A minnow seine not only produces a lot of bait, but is fun to use, especially in bays and tidal rivers. A seine is usually 4 feet high and anywhere from 10 to 50 feet long, with lead weights along the bottom and floats on top. A 20-footer is a good size for most purposes. Seining is easy. Two men carry the seine about 100 feet from shore or until depth hits 4 feet or so. Keeping the weighted end of the seine on the

Mike Sparano uses a drop or umbrella net. He'll lower it beneath the surface, sprinkle bread crumbs over it, and wait for bait fish to start feeding. Then he'll lift the net up fast and collect his bait.

Easier to use than nets is the minnow trap. Minnows swim into the funnel-like openings at either end, but can't find their way out. Set it near docks or wherever the current is weak. Bait it with a paste mix of oatmeal and water rolled into the size of a golfball.

120

Seiners work a stretch on a New Jersey Bay. Floats keep the top edge of the seine on the surface and lead weights keep the lower edge on the bottom.

With the seine on the beach, the fishermen collect their bait, which frequently includes spearing, sand eels, eels, crabs. An hour of seining is all it takes to collect enough bait for a day of fluke fishing and a night of striper fishing.

This 10-gallon bait can is aerated by battery and pump. Big bait containers with powered aerators come in handy when using big baits, such as live mackerel or herring for striped bass.

Lacking a battery-powered aerator for his minnows, Mike Sparano scoops up a canful of water and pours it back into the bucket from a height of two feet. Do this 12 times every 15 minutes or so and you'll provide enough oxygen for your bait.

bottom, the men sweep toward shore. The seine will belly out, catching everything in its path and carrying bait fish up on shore, where it can be picked up.

The next problem is keeping the minnows alive and fresh. The water must be aerated to keep enough oxygen in the bucket for survival, and this can be done in several ways. Water can be aerated by battery-powered devices. You can also aerate the water manually with a tin can.

Scoop up a canful of water and pour it back into the bucket from a height of 2 feet. Doing this 12 times every 15 minutes should provide sufficient oxygen for 24 minnows.

Bait water must be kept at a constant temperature. In summer, add ice cubes to the water before transporting them. As the ice melts, it will cool the water and add oxygen. Take care, however, not to cool the water too fast with ice.

It is important to avoid abrupt temperature changes, which will kill minnows.

If you plan to troll, keep bait in a bucket designed for trolling. This bucket, built to float on its side, will take water at an angle and aerate it.

If you're a stillfisherman, use the traditional bucket, which is actually two buckets. The outer bucket is used when transporting minnows.

This minnow bucket is of traditional design. The entire bucket is used when transporting bait. When you start fishing, lift out the insert and let it float upright in the water. Water will be changed constantly through the vents and bait will stay fresh. Avoid abrupt water temperature changes, however.

This trolling bucket makes it possible to keep your bait in the water while boat is moving. It floats on its side, as shown, and has openings to aerate water.

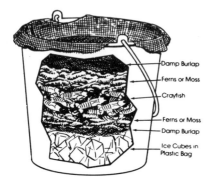

Damp Burlap
Ferns or Moss
Crayfish
Ferns or Moss
Damp Burlap
Ice Cubes in Plastic Bag

Crayfish Bucket—Bucket for cray-fish and crabs will keep bait fresh as long as it is cooled by ice and burlap is kept wet.

When you start fishing, lift out the insert and lower it into the water. The insert, which floats upright, is vented so that water is constantly changed.

Crawfish make excellent bait, but they can sometimes be difficult to find. I've had my best luck at night along gravelly shorelines. Crawfish feed in the shallows and you can spot them with a flashlight. Their eyes reflect red in the beam. When you locate one, hold a dip net behind it and touch its head with your hand or stick. If you're lucky, it will swim backward into the net. If you're fast, you can try grabbing a crawfish from behind with your hand.

Keeping crawfish fresh in hot weather can be a problem. I use an "ice bucket" set-up. In the bottom of a pail, I place 24 ice cubes in a plastic bag. I cover the ice with a layer of burlap, followed by a few inches of moss or ferns. Next I spread out the crawfish, which I cover with another layer of moss or ferns. I cover this top layer with another piece of wet burlap. Crawfish will stay in fine shape in this insulated pail during the hottest weather. Remember to keep that top piece of burlap wet.

Few anglers will question the value of a lively frog as a bait. Look for them along the grassy banks of creeks, ponds, and lakes. Catching them is not hard. You can catch a fair number during the day, but you can collect more at night with a flashlight and a long-handled small-mesh net. Frogs will remain still in the beam of a flashlight and you should have no trouble netting them.

Keeping a day's supply of frogs is no problem. The Oberlin Canteen Company makes a frog box or carrier. Or you can make your own.

I've covered only the popular baits. As you collect these baits, you'll soon discover that there is a great variety of other baits available. Sometimes catching the bait is as much fun as the fishing.

Frog Box—This frog box is easy to build and works fine. A knee-length sock, tacked to the furring strips, is a handle as well as a port for putting in and taking out frogs. Twist the sock to close it, and frogs cannot get out. If you leave the box overnight, weight the open end with stone.

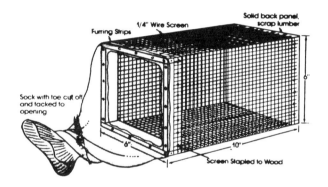

Panfishing teaches youngsters the fine art of cleaning—as well as catching —fish that are good table fare.

Even a neophyte can find fast action if he knows the rudiments of angling, as Tommy Russell proves here.

The Popular Panfish

BILL VOGT

Some writers consider panfish to be any fish too small to be classed as a gamefish, but I'd rather just say that panfish are fish without frills, fish that provide an angler with day-to-day satisfactions from the lake or stream nearest his home. I'm including not only the bluegill, crappie, yellow perch, and the other "usual" panfish, but the catfish, freshwater drum, and carp as well. In effect, panfish are anything you want them to be, excluding gamefish such as trout, black bass, muskie, pike, and walleye.

Panfishing has been called a kid's game, a good way to introduce neophytes to the basics of angling. At the other end of the pole, there are those who would have you believe that each of the 9 or 10 kinds of sunfish, for example, has its own special requirements as to tackle, bait or lures, and techniques. Actually, panfishing probably hits somewhere between the two—panfish can be remarkably choosy at times, but they're so plentiful that you can generally catch a few, if you know some rudiments of angling. To consistently catch the largest specimens, however, you'll need to use somewhat more sophisticated methods than did the mythical barefoot boy with willow stick and bent pin-and-worm.

Surprisingly, panfish often are underfished, and as many of these fish are prolific spawners, a body of water can soon be overrun with stunted fish that offer little sport or challenge. That's why so many states have liberal daily catch limits and no closed seasons on most species of panfish.

Tackle can range from a cane or telescoping glass pole to a light fly-casting rig or ultralight spinning outfit. I've caught a lot of bluegills, for example, on the same 7½-foot fly rod that I use for streamfishing for trout. An ultralight open-face spinning outfit is more versatile, however, and brings out the best in scrappy little battlers like bluegills, sunfish, and rock bass. A pushbutton spincasting reel would be a good choice for a beginner or occasional fisherman, though a lot of expert fishermen use them as well.

I keep my terminal tackle, as the hooks, weights, and lures that go on the business end of my line are called, separated by type. By using this modular approach, if the fish I'm after happen to be thinking "minnow," I can pull out an assortment of spinners, tiny spoons, and plugs. Or I can do the same thing with bugs and poppers, tiny plastic worms, flies, or baitfishing gear. I used to carry an assortment of pipe-tobacco tins, each labelled with grease pencil, but now I have a full-size Adventurer tackle box that contains an assortment of "cassettes," lidded boxes identical on the outside but with different compartment arrangements inside. I have boxes labelled as follows: Spinners, Bugs and Poppers, Plugs and Jigs, Flies, and Bait.

In the "Spinners" box I have a wide variety of spinners in the smaller sizes, some with bucktails, others with beaded bodies of various shapes. I also have some red-and-white spoons and weedless silver spoons ranging up to 1 inch or so in size.

My "Bugs and Poppers" box contains tiny cork-or-plastic flyrod poppers with feathers and/or rubber "legs." Another favorite of mine is a little piece of sponge rubber tied to a hook. Thin rubber-band legs are inserted with a darning needle. These bugs don't look like much, but they're easy to make and are killers for most species of panfish. The lure starts to sink after a few casts, but a quick squeeze will wring out the water and the bug will ride high and relatively dry again.

The plugs I carry are miniatures of popular bass plugs ranging from rubber-skirted poppers to deep-divers with metal lips. I prefer a plug that floats at rest so I can stop my retrieve to float it over a threatening branch as I work the underwater snags so often frequented by crappies and other panfish. Most of my jigs run to red, yellow, black, and white with feathers, bucktail, or marabou. You can make a simple jig by pinching a split-shot on just behind the eye of a long-shanked hook. Behind that, you can tie in a clump of bucktail. Paint the shot with nail polish or model-airplane dope and you're in business. Retouch as the paint chips off in use.

Flies that will work for trout also will work for panfish, but to my notion, trout flies are too expensive and too fragile for such work. Instead, I tie up a bunch of wingless, chenille-bodied hackle flies in red, yellow, brown, black, and white in sizes 8–14. They're really very simple to make, as you don't have to fool with wings and such—any fly-tying instruction book will show you how. I also have lots of streamers in the same colors. One of the most deadly "patterns" is simply a bit of

Arty Vogt, age six, can use ultralight rig, but his hands are too small for standard-size reel.

Modular approach to tackle utilizes cassette-loading tacklebox like this one by Vlchek Plastics.

Matt Sparano (right) and his brother Michael admire catch of platter-sized panfish.

silver or gold mylar tubing slipped over the hook and tagged fore and aft with red nylon thread. I also tie in a few strands of white or brown bucktail to give a streamer effect. I find these to be as good (and considerably cheaper) as the deadly Muddler Minnow and other popular patterns. When I'm fly fishing for panfish, I seldom use a tapered leader—a 6-foot hunk of 2-pound-test monofilament works fine.

Flyfishing purists will shudder, but when I was a youngster, I used to pull feathers from a pillow, tie them onto a hook, and I caught more sunfish than any boy I knew.

My baitfishing "module" is an assortment of red-and-white snap-on bobbers, some cork floats, and some slender quill-type bobbers. Hooks range from No. 6 to No. 12 in short and long shank. Thin-wire dry-fly hooks are the best because they're the least visible and cause the least damage to the bait. I also carry snelled bait-gripper hooks with serrated shanks. For weights (I prefer to fish without them whenever possible) I have thin wrap-around strips of lead, some egg-shaped sinkers with a

130

hole through the center, and several sizes of split-shot. The shot with little ears that you can pinch together to open the slit work best, as you can take them off or put them on at will.

For a worm box, I use a half-gallon milk carton. I wash it out, put in some worms and damp worm bedding or sphagnum moss (available at florists' shops), then staple the top shut. When I'm ready to fish, I cut a lid lengthwise in the carton. For a minnow bucket, it's hard to beat a Styrofoam beer cooler, six-pack size.

Action is often fast when you get into a school of panfish, and a mesh livebag with a floating ring can save a lot of time and will keep your fish fresher than a conventional stringer. You just unhook your fish, drop it in, and get your line out again as fast as you can. If a fish swallows a hook, simply snip the line and tie on another. The hook or lure can be recovered later, but a school of fish won't wait around while you wrestle with a swallowed hook.

SUNFISHES

Sunfishes, including the bluegill (called bream in the South) are doubtless the most popular of panfish. There are all sorts of hybrids and strains of bluegills and other sunfishes, including new fast-growing crosses that are being stocked by a number of state conservation agencies. Florida beam, like Florida bass, are being imported by some states to see if they will grow as fast outside their home environment.

Bluegills will attack just about anything they can cram into their mouths, any they often don't stop at that. I've had a bluegil hit the trailing hook of a three-gang muskie plug, and they'll often nip at a pork rind or the rubber skirt of a bass plug.

Bluegills weighing more than 4 pounds have been caught, but a fat 8-incher is a good catch in anyone's book. You'll generally find the smaller bluegills hugging the shallows during the day, with the larger ones hanging back in deeper water. You best chances of hooking a big one are early in the morning and just at dusk. A small flyrod popper or rubber-legged sponge-bodied bug is deadly, as is a small spinner with a fly for a trailer.

One of my favorite lures is a spinning-size pork rind on a bare long-shank No. 8 hook. I either flycast or use an ultralight spinning outfit.

Same tactics that work for panfish also catch bass, as Vin T. Sparano shows.

You just cast it out and let it flutter down. Often, you'll see a flash of white as the rind takes off for parts unknown. If you don't get a hit, let the rind rest on the bottom for a few moments, then give it a twitch and let it flutter down again.

Other sunfish, including the green sunfish, the shellcracker or redear, and the pumpkinseed, tend to favor insects and small crustacea and are more readily caught on flies. If you don't have a flyfishing outfit, you can clip a plastic bubble or bobber onto a spinning line and have good sport, though it's a bit awkward to retrieve a fly effectively in this manner.

132

Giby Russell and fish from a New York pond.

Bluegill is one of the most fished-for panfish because it's a hard fighter and will take artificials as well as bait. (Photo courtesy Nebraska Game Commission)

WARMOUTH AND ROCK BASS

Warmouth and rock bass are quite similar in appearance (see the table at the end of this chapter), but the warmouth prefers mud bottoms and quiet waters, while the rock bass likes cooler, clearer water—much the same sort of environment preferred by smallmouth bass.

Floatfishing is a popular way of taking rock bass, or redeye, and I've caught a good many of them that way in the New River in Virginia. My favorite bait is a nightcrawler. I cast a bit upstream and let the unweighted bait drift along with the boat until the current drags unnaturally against the line. A small yellow wobbling plug also works well, once you learn to keep it pulling against the current at just the right speed to bring out the action. Driftfishing for rock bass is a delightful, quiet way to spend a day, and there's always the chance that a big buster of a bass will smash into your lure or bait for a change of pace.

Nice catch of sunnies from pond in New York's Catskill Mountains.

White crappie is sometimes known as papermouth because of its tender mouth. (Photo courtesy Nebraska Game Commission)

CRAPPIES

I grew up fishing for crappies in the backwaters of the Missouri River, and like most people who angle for old papermouth, as crappies sometimes are called, I'd rate a small minnow as the best bait. I've never done too well with crappies on flies, though a smallish streamer occasionally has given me some fast action. Weighted bucktail spinners and small jigs can work wonders on these black-spotted silvery fish. One of my favorite tactics with artificials is to use a 12-foot telescoping glass pole (mine is a St. Croix, but there are several manufacturers producing such poles) and a small red-bodied jig. I sweep the jig among the rocks and underwater debris along the riprap that separates the sloughs from the main river. In lakes, I use an ultralight spinning outfit and cast over submerged brushpiles and downed trees.

Like most fish of the sunfish family, crappies are notorious school fish, and you can expect fast action for a time. When the action slows, you have to begin prospecting all over again. Some fishermen take one crappie and tie a balloon or bobber to a line that's secured to the fish's dorsal fin. They release the fish so it will run with the school, betraying its presence like a Judas goat that led lambs to slaughter.

White bass is a popular school-fish on reservoirs. (Photo courtesy Nebraska Game Commission)

WHITE AND YELLOW BASS

Both of these fish bear some resemblance to the striped bass of salt water. Yellows have a limited distribution and are found mostly in the Missouri–Mississippi River system along rocky shoals and gravel bars. White bass are an open-water fish, and have been widely stocked in reservoirs.

I've fished for bass in Lake McConaughy in Nebraska and the Lake of the Ozarks in Missouri. Fish weighing 1 pound or more give a good account of themselves on light tackle. Minnows, especially shad, are fine fare for white bass, as are small spoons, spinners, and streamers.

On large bodies of water, you can spot a school of white bass by watching the gulls. Often, the bass will corner a school of minnows and drive them to the surface, which in turn triggers a feeding spree among the gulls, who wheel around and around, skimming low to snipe at the already confused baitfish.

In the spring, you'll find schools of whites migrating up the lake's feeder streams. You can follow the shoreline or drift in a boat and catch as many white bass as you want—sometimes more than you can use. I've seen fishermen bring in garbage cans full of white bass from Lake McConaughy. I've no quarrel with this, provided the fish are used, but I don't think I'd enjoy fishing very much if my main objective were to fill my freezer.

YELLOW PERCH

The yellow perch is kin to the walleye and sauger, but it's considerably smaller—a 2-pounder is a good one. This fish doesn't do well in warm or weedy water and is primarily a lake-dweller. Perch tend to stay in fairly deep water and generally feed only during daylight hours. Minnows, crawfish, and worms are the best baits, and spoons and spinners rate highest among artificials.

Perch bite readily in winter and are extremely popular among ice fishermen. The lakes of Wisconsin and Michigan, for example, sprout veritable villages of ice-fishing shanties each year, and the cult is growing. In winter, the best bait for perch is often perch. The eyes from a freshly caught perch are killers, and a strip cut from a perch's belly also works well at times when you jig it up and down. Almost any kind of grub is also an effective bait.

An ice fisherman's array of gear includes a spud or sharpened piece of axle to chip out a hole (or if you're really into this kind of fishing, you'll probably buy a power-driven auger). You'll also need a perforated skimmer to scoop the slush from the hole; one of those large serving spoons with a slotted bowl can be scrounged from the kitchen for the purpose. Some ice fishermen run strings of holes, much like a trapline, with tip-ups (a flag-bearing crosspiece of wire or wood that snaps upright when there's a fish on), but I prefer to fish on a one-to-one basis, a hole at a time.

BULLHEADS

Most fishermen need no introduction to brown, yellow, and black bullheads. Bullheads are among the hardiest fish known to man. They can be dug with pitchforks from the bottom muck of a dried-up pond, and they can survive in all but the most polluted water. They are slow, steady biters and will take your bait clear down to their gullets if you let them.

Bullheads eat virtually anything, but I've never seen one caught on an artificial lure. I like to use a big gob of nightcrawlers with a weight

137

Bullhead is easy to catch, but beware of its spines. (Photo courtesy Nebraska Game Commission)

at the end of my line. If I'm using two hooks, I tie them fairly far apart, as one fish may inhale one bait, hook and all, then move on to the next if you don't reel him in soon enough. You can put your line in and sit patiently waiting for a bullhead to come along, but I prefer to retrieve the line, about ½ inch at a time, dragging the bait ever so slowly across the bottom. Often, a bullhead will bite with a staccato series of jerks. Once he starts biting, it would take a stick of dynamite to make him stop, unless you get excited and reel in too soon.

Bullheads, like other catfish, feed best at night, and I've spent many an hour along a Midwestern river, listening to the night sounds as I tended my line. Where it's legal, you can put out a number of bank-lines, go to bed, and then come back in the morning to retrieve your catch. There's a certain satisfaction in knowing that those lines are out there, working for you as you sleep.

CATFISH

I've never outgrown my fascination for catfish—either the channel cat with its light-colored, streamlined body or the ugly flathead, a fish that looks like an overgrown bullhead.

My earliest recollections of angling are of days when I chased after my cousin, Bob Barnard, as he and his friends wound their way through Iowa cornfields on their way to the Missouri River or the Little Sioux in search of a likely catfish hole. Bob is one of those rare men who learns to think like the fish they catch. He uses the grossest kinds of bait you can imagine, but he maintains he's a trout fisherman at heart and a practicing catfisherman by circumstance simply because Iowa is not exactly the trout capital of the world.

One of Bob's favorite methods is to stalk his quarry with a fly rod, much like a trout fisherman. The only difference is that on the business end of his line is a piece of chicken gut. The hook does not pierce the gut, but is threaded through the hollow center. When about 8 inches of gut are strung onto the line, Bob snips off the end with a pair of scissors. He half-hitches the upper end, line and all. About 6 inches above this he ties a sinker. He walks along the stream until he comes to a snag that's been ditched out by the current. He lets the gut work down under the

Catfish expert Bob Barnard (left) and party of trotliners took these flat-heads from Missouri River.

snag, where it waves back and forth. A big channel cat will hit this with no preliminaries, and if you aren't ready, you stand a good chance of losing your rod. The bad part of this kind of fishing is the handling of the gut, and the stench that permeates your clothes as the day wears on. The good part is that a piece of gut will last for hours, and you don't have to rebait often. If you're finicky, you can carry a piece of wire to pull the hook through the gut, which saves some handling.

Bob uses the same stalk-and-fish method with a variety of baits. One of them—I'm not sure it's made anymore—is a tan concoction that comes in a jar labelled "Bowker's Catfish Bait." One sniff separates the men from the boys, but Bob avoids even touching the stuff by carrying a pocketful of sponges cut into squares. He hooks on a sponge and swishes it around in the jar with a stick. This technique also works with another of Bob's favorites, a tightly packed jar of minnows that has been out in the sun for a few days.

For the faint of heart, there are other, less odoriferous ways of catching channel catfish. Channels will hit a plug on occasion. I've caught them on a yellow wobbler retrieved very slowly. Or you can cast nightcrawlers or gizzard shad into the tailwaters of a dam and let the current bump the bait along the bottom. Catfish congregate in such places, attracted by the baitfish that are chopped up and spewed out by the power-generating turbines. The flathead catfish is considerably uglier than the channel cat, but its eating habits appear to be infinitely tidier. I've never caught a flathead on chicken entrails or anything dead, for example. A live nightcrawler or a struggling bluegill have worked best for me, but I suppose a few flatheads *are* caught on coagulated hog blood, entrails, chicken liver, or any of the other popular channel-catfish baits.

CARP

One of the beauties of defining panfish as "fish without frills" is that you can include just about anything that strikes your fancy, which is why I've added the carp.

Carp were imported into the United States from Europe in the 1800's —a tragic mistake, as it turned out, for this prolific spawner spread like wildfire, disrupting the habitat and spawning beds of other species. In

Matt Sparano displays carp that gave a good account of itself on spincasting outfit.

some areas, the carp has roiled the water so much with its hoglike rooting that it has ruined the feeding grounds of waterfowl and shorebirds. But now, we're stuck with the carp, so we might as well get what enjoyment we can out of it.

I remember one encounter with carp that took place on a small pond in Omaha, Nebraska. I was fly fishing for bluegills without much success, when I saw some big carp sucking up a storm on the surface under a big tree that leaned out from the bank. I slipped up for a closer look, and saw that it was a mulberry tree. I could see the carps' mouths working as they fed. Their extended, tubular sucking lips made little kissing noises as they ate mulberries that had fallen from the tree.

I snipped off my fly and tied on a No. 10 thin-wire hook. I put some of the berries in a paper cup I found nearby, and I climbed the tree. By leaning out over the water, I was able to lower the berry to where the fish were feeding. *Wham.* A fish sucked the berry up without hesitation and I set the hook. Climbing back down wasn't easy with the fish on, but I managed it without too much trouble. I brought the carp in after a hard, lunging fight that didn't do my fly rod any good. I let the water rest for 30 minutes, then went back. I repeated the process several times and caught four of the big bronze pug-uglies, each weighing between 5 and 6 pounds.

Carp are fond of canned peas, corn, Ivory soap, and stale bread moistened and molded around a treble hook. Another favorite bait is doughball. You can make a good standard doughball by mixing a little water, ¼ cup of corn syrup, and 2 cups of corn meal. Roll it into a big ball and wrap it in a rag. Put the whole thing into boiling water and cook it until it has a rubbery consistency. Some fishermen mix in some shreds of cotton to help keep the bait together on the hook. Pinch off pieces as you need them.

I use a No. 10 treble hook with a little coil spring on the shank. I press the doughball into place and mold it into a teardrop shape, covering all three points of the hook. The spring helps hold the doughball in place. Use as little weight as possible, as the carp has a very sensitive mouth and will drop the bait at the first sign that all is not well.

FRESHWATER DRUM

The freshwater drum is a peculiar fish—it's the only freshwater representative of its family. It has the arched back that's typical among its saltwater relatives, and its otoliths, or ear bones, were used as wampum by Indians. When I was a boy, I used to save these bones as "lucky stones."

The drum, which also goes by the intriguing name, "gaspergou," is one of those fish you usually catch by chance, when you're fishing for something else, such as crappies.

Freshwater drum is usually caught when angler is fishing for something else. (Photo courtesy Nebraska Game Commission)

The drum is a clean-looking silvery fish with a curved lateral line that sweeps from the gill covers to the tip of the tail. It has rasping teeth and feeds on freshwater clams, snails, and minnows.

The fish isn't bad eating, though it's a bit bony. In Wisconsin, fisheries biologists urge anglers to keep any drum they catch, as the fish has taken over a number of lakes there, crowding out more desirable species. The flesh has a high protein content, and it's often caught commercially and sold as mink food.

OTHER "FISH WITHOUT FRILLS"

My list of fish without frills goes on and on. It includes mooneyes and skipjacks I might tie into by chance while fishing for sauger in the tailrace at Gavins Point Dam on the Missouri River, slender alligator gar that fight like a snake gone mad, and suckers, chubs, and overgrown goldfish that may be fugitives from someone's aquarium.

I remember one delightful afternoon on the Willowemoc River in New York. I'd come in high excitement at the prospect of fishing this fabled trout stream that has been extolled by generations of anglers and described in many of the literary classics of the sport. After hours of fruitless casting, I caught and released one fish, an utterly useless fallfish, which is a minnow resembling a creek chub. Then I caught another. And another. Backsliding purist that I am, I soon reverted to my baser instincts and dared to enjoy it. To me, it's not so much what kind of fish you catch that counts. I have a deep and abiding appreciation for *any* fish that happens to get onto the hook end of my line. If it happens to be a fish without frills, so be it.

SOME COMMON "FISH WITHOUT FRILLS"

SUNFISH FAMILY

Bluegill: Like others of its family, the bluegill's coloration can be quite faded under certain water conditions. Generally, olive on back and bluish on the sides and under the gills. The breast can range from white to orange.

Pumpkinseed: Has vertical greenish bars on the sides with irregular reddish spots, but markings can vary greatly from region to region. The give-away is a bright orange spot on the rear tip of the gill-plate. Belly varies from orange to rust.

Green Sunfish: Has a large mouth and resembles a smallmouth bass in general outline. Back is olive-green. Underside is pale yellow. Has light lines on gill plates. Often found in siltier water than its relatives can tolerate.

Orangespotted Sunfish: Generally distinguished by irregular orange blotches on the sides, this is one of the smallest sunfish and it seldom exceeds 5 inches in length.

Redear Sunfish, or Shellcracker: Resembles the pumpkinseed, but a sure way to tell is to flex the gill cover. If it bends, you have a redear, if it's rigid, a pumpkinseed. Very popular among Southern anglers.

Longear Sunfish: A relatively small fish, the longear is named for the elongated ear flap on the tip of its gill covering. The fish's sides are flecked with yellow.

Yellowbreast Sunfish, or Redbreast: An Eastern fish, the Yellowbreast has an elongated black flap at the tip of its gill cover. Often has yellowish sides and a bright orange belly.

Spotted Sunfish, or Stumpknocker: A small fish, seldom exceeding 6 inches, the spotted sunfish has an olive-green body specked with brown and black.

White Crappie: The top of the head has a dished-out appearance, and the fish's silvery sides are generally marked with bands of black dots. Prefers siltier water than its close relative, the black crappie (see below). Has 6 spines on the dorsal fin.

Black Crappie: Black markings are more irregular than on the white crappie, and the dorsal fin has 7 or 8 spines. Sometimes the only way you can tell a black crappie from a white is by counting the spines. Both fish have tender mouths and sometimes are called papermouths. A landing net is a good idea, as a hook will tear free easily.

Warmouth: Unlike the rock bass, which it resembles, the warmouth prefers mud bottoms and weedy, sluggish water. Color varies from gray to olive-green, and the body structure somewhat resembles that of a smallmouth bass. The eyes are reddish. A sure way to tell a warmouth from a rock bass is to run your finger over its tongue. If it has tiny serrated teeth, it's a warmouth.

Rock Bass: The rock bass has no teeth on its tongue (see warmouth, above). It prefers cool water and is often found in rivers with rocky or gravelly beds.

144

THE POPULAR PANFISH

White Bass: A silvery fish with yellowish tint on belly. Has about 10 unbroken dark stripes on the side (as contrasted with the yellow bass's six or seven broken stripes). The white bass is widely stocked in large impoundments.

Yellow Bass: Not nearly so widely distributed as the white bass, the yellow bass is a native of the lower Mississippi River drainage and Texas. The fish has broken stripes on its sides (see white bass, above).

PERCH FAMILY

Yellow Perch: Body is elongated and mostly greenish yellow with about 6 dark bands running about halfway down the sides. Has rows of small teeth.

CROAKER FAMILY

Freshwater Drum: The only freshwater representative of its family, the drum has a rounded tail and a humped back. Can grow to more than 50 pounds, but 2- to 3-pounders are the most common. Ranges from the Missouri River to the Atlantic Coast and from Canada to the Gulf of Mexico. Depending upon habitat, the drum's coloration can be milky white, gray, or bright silver.

MINNOW FAMILY

Carp: Carp are silvery when young and turn golden-yellow or dark bronze as they mature. Scales are very large, and the tubular mouth sports fleshy barbels. Can grow to more than 50 pounds.

CATFISH FAMILY

Channel Catfish: Younger fish have dark flecks on their silvery sides. Tail is deeply forked. Often has been billed as the "sportiest" of its clan, but will eat carrion. Also hits artificial lures with some regularity.

Flathead Catfish, or Mud Catfish: Has flat, wide head with protruding lower jaw. The tail is not deeply notched, and the flathead is not nearly as streamlined in appearance as the channel catfish.

Bullheads (brown, black, and yellow): Bullheads have large heads, wide mouths, and rounded tails. Color is your best guide to distinguishing the three fish. All have white-to-yellowish bellies and darker upper surfaces. The yellow bullhead generally has bright yellow underparts. Bullheads answer to a variety of names, including horned pout, catfish, and mudcat. The sharp spines on the dorsal and pectoral surfaces can inflict a painful wound, especially if it's a young fish.

Mangrove roots, like these, are a hideout for the baitfish living on the flats. Predatory fish, especially snook and snapper, often go there to feed—a well placed cast sometimes takes a nice fish.

Fishing the Flats

LEFTY KREH

Perhaps the most exciting light-tackle fishing of all is to stalk the shallow saltwater flats of the warmer seas, searching for bonefish, tarpon, permit, mutton snapper, barracuda, and many other predatory fishes, capable of tremendous speed.

Fishes that roam the flats in search of their food are away from their protective cover, and they become extremely nervous, wary, and will flee at the slightest sign of danger.

One of the most difficult of all fishes to approach in extremely shallow water, less than 18 inches in depth, is the shark. A shark in 10 to 100 feet of water is afraid of very little, often allowing you to motor directly over it without disturbing the fish.

But, place that same shark in water that barely covers his dorsal fin and he becomes a different sort. A boat pole rubbing against the side of the boat, a foot that scrapes on the deck, even a heavy fly line dropping to the surface on a cast can frighten a 100-pound shark completely off the flats.

You must always be aware of the sounds created by the fisherman and the guide. I don't mean talking, but any sounds that can be communicated through the boat. Opening a cooler to get a beer, then dropping the lid, can spoil acres of flats. Dropping a pair of pliers on the

Lefty Kreh and son, Larry, working the flats for bonefish. This is a typical small skiff, Lefty is standing on a casting platform, while Larry is elevated on the storage box for better visibility.

boat deck, sliding a chair or tackle box across the deck, stamping your feet, all these sounds are foreign to the fish that are prowling the flats—and while they may not flee, they will be on their guard.

What is a flat?

A flat is a shallow saltwater area directly against the shore in most cases, although some very shallow flats are created where humps of land rise to within a few feet of the ocean's surface, sometimes miles from land. But, most of the time, a flat is the shallows near an island or mainland, which connects the land area to the deeper water.

The flats are also adjacent to the deeper water where the predatory fishes we hope to catch live and seek shelter from their enemies. They vary in depth, and what depth you fish in for specific species is vital information.

These flats are really the dining tables of the predatory species. Their living room and bedroom is the reef line or nearby depths. But most of the time their food is obtained on the shallow shelfs that rise from the depths.

Flats vary in size, location, hardness and softness of the bottom, types of grasses and animal life that live on them, even in the type of material forming the base. The base may be pure sand, a marl, or almost solid rock.

Learning to recognize the variables on a flat is important. An experienced bonefish guide can tell you at a glance that many flats will not be as productive as others—perhaps only a few hundred yards away.

Turtle grass is a choice vegetation on productive saltwater flats. It resembles wide blades of lawn grass, perhaps ½ to ⅝ inches wide, and can vary in length from several inches to nearly two feet long in most places. But generally it will range in length from 4 to 12 inches.

This medium-to dark-green grass is a sign of a healthy flat that should possess lots of worms, crustaceans, crabs, shrimp, and other good things that some of the predatory fish like to eat.

Bare rock flats are usually poor for fishing. They may, however, be a highway between one productive flat and another. Fish could possibly have to swim over this flat in order to get to another hotspot. So, while rocky flats deserve second consideration, when compared to those filled with turtle grass, never ignore any flat before examining it at different tides.

How much grass is on a flat determines to some extent what kind of fish you'll find there. For example, flats that have very little grass will usually be devoid of sea trout, for the sea trout feeds on the minnow life that seeks shelter in the grass.

Redfish, called channel bass farther north, roam many of the flats from the Keys near Islamorada, all the way up the Gulf of Mexico coast into Texas. Again, they feed almost exclusively where a rich growth of grass has taken hold. Often you will see a redfish worming through the shallows with its entire body beneath the stems. In fact, if a redfish is approached and it figures it's too late to run, it will settle into the grass in such a manner that it will actually disappear as you watch it.

Permit like a flat that is usually pretty hard, one that has a lot of small stones on it—but some grass, too. A hotspot on a flat for permit, one that you should always check out if permit are likely to be in that area, is all rocky outcroppings which are surrounded by turtle grass.

The vey best bait for permit is a crab, here is how you hook a blue crab —note claws have been removed to aid in hooking fish.

Lefty Kreh with a nice 32-pound permit taken on 10-pound-test spinning line and a crab for a bait.

Crabs seek shelter in rocky crevices, where they can back in, raise a pair of snapping claws at an intruder, and be safe. Crabs are to permit what candy and ice cream are to children—something neither of them can ignore. Thus, permit that feed on particular flats a great deal know from experience that they can expect to find the crabs hiding in the rocky shelter.

Charts will often indicate likely rocky spots, since they are marked on these charts to alert the boater—but they can also tip off the fisherman. I know of several fine permit areas close to busy marinas that seem ignored. Yet, I found these flats through charts that showed where channels had been constructed and the rocky base had been tossed to the side, forming another dining room table for the permit.

If you fish for permit on flats containing little rock shelf or outcroppings, your first consideration is water depth. I have seen on three occasions where a permit, obviously in pursuit of food, got into water so shallow that it turned over on its side and swam after the meal as if it were a flounder. But that can be considered an abnormal characteristic.

150

Most of the time a permit wants to swim upright, where it is in command of its total faculties. That means when you seek permit you should not try to work waters less than 18 inches. Water to 4 feet is not too deep to work for permit, and I prefer depths from about 2 to 3 feet as ideal.

Mutton snapper, which are brightly colored snappers of the reef line, invade some flats, too. And while fishermen rave about permit as being shy, I consider the mutton snapper to be the most wary—as do many other experienced flats anglers.

I feel that one of the greatest catches I ever made was an 18-pound mutton snapper on a fly. The mutton snapper generally feeds in water depths the same as the permit, but rarely do you find mutton snapper on a flat that is not directly connected to the ocean or the main body of water in that region. Apparently, they come from the reef area to feed briefly, then return.

The only time I know that mutton snappers can be found with regularity is in May, when they move up on some of the flats in the extreme lower end of the Florida Keys, and on some of the flats in the Yucatan Peninsula, we think, to spawn. Often they will be following a muddying ray (a sting ray that is pounding the muddy bottom with its wings to flush food) and a cast to the mutton snapper then will draw the best strikes from this extremely wary fish.

But, there will be no mutton snappers on those flats unless the water depth is correct—from 2 to 4 feet.

Tarpon can be found on all sorts of flats—because there are all sorts of sizes of this grand fish. If you like to fish baby tarpon in the mangroves, generally a high tide will find them clustered under the spiderlike roots and overhanging foliage. But if you want to catch a big tarpon, one at least 60 or 70 pounds in weight, you must seek the fish in deeper waters.

Tarpon can be fished many ways, and a whole book could be devoted to the subject. I am going to generalize, only because space limits the subject. The bigger tarpon in the Florida Keys move into the lower portion sometime in January or February, depending upon the winter chill. In warm winters they will appear around Key West in numbers in January. Then slowly, as the numbers of tarpon come in from the depths increase, they will begin moving up through the Mud Keys, Snipe Keys, behind Sugarloaf Keys, and up to the Bahia Honda Channel

151

Lefty Kreh holds up a tarpon he landed on the fly tackle held aloft by his companion, Harold LeMaster of Clearwater, Florida.

and nearby flats. Some also work very early into the Yacht Channel area near Long Key.

What is surprising, and no one seems to know why, is that these big tarpon move into what is termed among local fishermen and guides as the backcountry. The backcountry is the Florida Bay area, lying to the west and north, or on the right as you travel the highway down through the Keys.

These tarpon move onto the banks, which are really flats, generally richly covered with turtle grass, with a water depth of from 4 to 10 feet.

Often these fish are most difficult to see, under even the best of conditions. Tarpon have a dark green back, and when they swim along, down several feet below the surface, cruising over the rich, dark green turtle grass, they become almost invisible.

Most alert fishermen who work the flats know that most predatory fishes that feed on the flats have silvery-colored sides. When you pull such a fish from the water, you wonder how you could possibly not have seen this fish as it swam along. If you consider that a tarpon appears almost to be coated in wet aluminum paint when first pulled from the

152

water, you are amazed that a silvery fish 6 feet in length was not visible as it cruised over a dark green bed of turtle grass.

The answer is obvious, however. That silvery side of the tarpon, bonefish, barracuda, snapper, permit, and others, acts exactly like a mirror. As it swims over a dark, green bottom, that exact shade is reflected to the viewer. When it moves to a lighter flats floor, the same color continues to be reflected, making it one of nature's most perfect forms of camouflage. That's why it is impossible to see a school of striped bass in the shallows—the whole school is reflecting the bottom back to the fisherman.

Sea trout like to feed on the flats or in shallow basins on a flat where the water is at least 3 feet deep. Bonefish are different. If there's enough water to aid them in pushing their body along in search of food, bonefish will often go there to feed. Some outdoor writers have written that an incoming tide on a flat is the very best time to fish for bonefish. That's not really true.

Each flat must be taken as an individual dining table. Flats that border the ocean, or a deep channel that drains directly into the depths, are often best on incoming tide. The reason for this, of course, is that bonefish live in the depths, and as the water rises on the flats, the places close to their shelter and home will be the first flats they will move onto.

Flats a little farther away from the depths will be dry at low tide, and will be receiving their water much later in the tide phase. The creatures on the flats that are mobile, such as shrimp and crabs, know that the predatory fishes will feed as the tide rises, and they often retreat in numbers before the rising water.

A nice bonefish, taken on a ¼-ounce jig.

For that reason, bonefish are often seen feeding in water so shallow that their backs protrude above the surface as they race the rising water attempting to catch the food that is staying in the shallowest areas.

That means that as the tide rises (later in the tidal stage) the bonefish will be feeding just as avidly way back on the flat, or flats that are located farther from the depths and are just getting their rising water.

The very top of the tide may be the best time to fish on some flats, for only on the upper limits of a tide are some flats well covered, so the bonefish can feed there.

The falling tide is another tide that can furnish superior fishing on some flats. As the tide races back to deeper water, the crabs, shrimp, and other food delay going with that tide until they can no longer remain in their shallow-water shelter. Thus bonefish will often prowl in extremely shallow water on a flat, catching the very last stage of a falling tide and the food that is swept to it.

Therefore, no particular stage of any tide can be said to be the best tide for bonefish or other flats fishes. Each flat must be analyzed on its own merits, such as its location and how the tide affects it.

It is also important to know that some flats have a certain sector that will hold feeding fish on specific tides, but that the same flats may also be good on another tidal phase. Or that one flat, or a portion of a flat, is always productive, while other parts of the same flat, or nearby flats that resemble the productive areas will usually be empty of fish.

I suppose that you could never overstate the fact that when you first fish any flat you should have a guide for at least the first time or two you fish there. The guide knows the productive flats and the tide phases to fish those flats—information that simply takes a lot of time to absorb.

How you approach a flat is also important. On some large flats this doesn't make any difference, but it can mean success or failure in many cases.

I fished Key West with Captain Bill Curtis several times. Once, when making a film for ABC American Sportsman TV show, we were doing one on permit. I knew that Bill had outstanding success with permit in the Key West area. I also knew that many local fishermen did rather poorly, often during the same tide phases and on the same flats that Bill worked. What I didn't know until that time was that how you approach a flat is sometimes vital to success.

We were going to fish a permit flat near some very deep water, and

Bill explained exactly how he wanted to come up on that flat. He indicated that the permit would be lying in the deeper water, waiting for the tide to start falling. Then they would move up along the edge of the flat and wait for the crabs to be swept along the flat's edge.

It was extremely important to come up on that flat from the upper end, and not to motor over the side of the channel bordering the flat for fear of running the permit out of the area. His plan worked and we got all the permit we needed. It was my first lesson in approaching flats, and I never forgot it.

This same Bill Curtis, whom I regard as the best bonefish guide I have ever known, will race up to a flat in his home waters of Biscayne Bay and, with the throttle at near full bore, come to a roaring stop, pick up the anchor and heavy chain and throw it into the clear waters of the Bay with a tremendous splashing noise.

Why would he take so much care in one situation and seem so careless in another? Bill knew that the permit were in the deeper water and that running over them when they were so close to their feeding station along the flats edge would frighten them away. He also knows that the bonefish he intends to fish for in some situations are off in a distant portion of deep water and will be moving onto these flats from that deep water. Since he approached the fishing area from across the shallow flats, devoid at the time of fish, he did not frighten any bonefish, and because they are still some distance away, prior to moving into the area, he feels no need for excessive caution.

The whole example points up that it's a good idea to approach an area with caution when required, and that sometimes caution is not needed. But it also points up that when you are not sure, move into and out of an area with care.

One way of having every knowledgeable guide and tarpon fisherman ready to kill you is to work for giant tarpon in some of the basins and along the banks in the Keys—then, if you decide to leave, start up your motor and run full bore out of the. area. You'll earn the other fishermen's undying hate. Always move into an area where tarpon, stripers, or other wary fish feed with quiet caution—and leave the same way.

Knowing the movements of fish is also vital. For example, we've found that permit are perhaps on the flats in the most numbers in May. Yet, in June, they seem to disappear entirely. We have noticed that the permit will begin showing up around the wrecks in the Gulf of Mexico and other places in the Atlantic Ocean in large numbers in June, remaining a part of July, when most of the permit seem to leave the wrecks and their numbers again increase inshore on the flats.

This means that a sportsman from the North, whose desire is to catch a nice permit, would be foolish to book a trip to the flats in June.

The tarpon that move into the backcountry (Florida Bay) area of the Keys in the winter, and continue to build in numbers into April and May, for some strange reason all begin a movement to the oceanside in early May, remaining there in fair numbers through all of June and parts of July.

This mass migration in May has not been explained, but it's a regular event that is predictable. What it means to the fisherman is that he should learn where the giant tarpon are working certain banks in Florida Bay in April, for unless he is aware of the migration of these same fish to the ocean the following month, he could spend weeks in Florida Bay looking for fish that aren't there.

Temperature as well as seasonal changes can affect flats fishes, too. My choice months for bonefishing are May and October. Generally, in Florida and the Bahamas, the days are not yet blistering hot. The nights are cool, and so the waters on the very shallow flats where the bonefish feed do not heat up much during the day, making it too uncomfortable for them.

In much of April and May, as well as October and most of November (until the cold fronts start chilling the waters), the bonefish can be expected to remain on the flats all day. During the hotter summer months the bonefish will feed very early and late in the day, with midday fishing pretty skimpy.

In the winter months, chilly winds often lower the flats' water temperatures so much that the bonefish leave them entirely for several days. These cold periods are brief, but they can spoil your trip if you plan to fish for bonefish in the Keys in mid-winter.

In the Yucatan Peninsula area of Mexico and Belize, the water remains warm throughout the year. Bonefish here seem to be able to tolerate a higher water temperature and will often feed well through the summer day on flats that would be considered too warm.

A brief look at some of the temperatures that guides and anglers have established as the low points where fish will begin moving to the flats in numbers is worthwhile. Tarpon seem to prefer water temperatures on

Lefty Kreh with a nice shark taken on a fly rod.

the flats as low as 72 degrees. If it drops much below that they will generally retreat to deeper water.

Bonefish will be scarce when temperatures drop to 72, but a few will continue to feed until 70 degrees is hit—sometimes you'll see bonefish on the flats at 67 or 68 degrees, but they become very difficult to catch. Bonefish will feed well into the low 80's.

Permit and mutton snappers are more susceptible to chilly waters than bonefish. It takes about 74 degrees before permit become very active, and they can feed right into the mid-80's before it gets too warm for them.

Sharks are almost nonexistent when waters reach 74 degrees. They really leave the flats from the first serious cold spell in November, and won't come back until late March or even into late April, when waters reach 74 degrees or better. Hot weather doesn't seem to bother them, and they will often feed all day in August, with the dorsal fin a high black sailboat as they move across the flats in search of food.

Jim Maloney, Langdon, North Dakota, lifts a nice snook aboard that took a plastic tipped jig among the mangrove bushes in the Ten Thousand Island area.

Snook lie in white-colored pot holes in the flats in Florida Bay and along the Yucatan Peninsula. Here Larry Kreh shows one he took on a yellow and red streamer fly—their favorite color.

Sea trout like cooler weather and I've seen good sea trout fishing in shallow basins when water temperatures were in the low 60's, but I prefer water from about 65 to 72 degrees for sea trout.

Redfish can't seem to get water warm enough on the shallow water flats, and the month of August, with the warmest water temperatures of the year, sees the highest number of them feeding in the shallows.

Fishing tackle for working the flats varies, depending upon the type of fish and the size you seek. Obviously the gear needed to subdue a bonefish will not work well to take a giant tarpon.

Basically, you need two or three outfits to fish the flats. And, while fly fishing perhaps offers the most fun, and in some cases is the most effective tool, spinning gear is by far the best all-round fishing equipment.

For bonefish, mutton snapper of all kinds, smaller permit, small sharks, redfish, snook, and many other species, a spinning reel that will handle 4- to 8-pound line is ideal. The rod should be matched to handle lures from ⅛- to ½-ounce.

Fishing for the above mentioned species requires stealth to get in position to take the fish, and then usually a delicate but accurate presentation must be made. Heavy, bulky rods and noise-splashing lures are generally poor tools for this delicate work. Therefore, the lighter lines and more sensitive rods make for the best equipment.

You can also use light plug-casting gear—but it should have some sort of drag, since a line melting from the reel by a rapidly disappearing bonefish is nothing that you can put the thumb on to slow the reel spool.

Proper technique when stripping line on the retrieve with a fly is to keep the rod low and pointed toward the fish, using the hand to manipulate the fly—flipping the rod up and down to get action creates a lot of slack, making it difficult to set the hook on the strike.

Typical scene on a bonefish flat, angler, with fly rod high to prevent cut-offs from sharp coral allows the fish to make the first smoking run.

If you prefer fly tackle, a rod that will handle a weight-forward Size 8 or 9 is dandy for such work. It will deliver a fairly good-size fly to the target, and yet allow you a delicate presentation when required. It will also fight successfully just about any of the mentioned species of fish.

If you search for cobia around the shallow-water markers, where they often bask near the surface, or if you want to take a fairly large shark, tarpon or permit, you need a beefier rod for these bruisers.

Rods that have plenty of guts in the butt section, but will flex enough to handle the lures on the cast are desirable. What you don't want is a rod that is powerful in the rear portion, but has a floppy tip, often referred to as a fast-action rod. Such rods will fight fish well, but the floppy tip makes it almost impossible to manipulate a surface lure to bring out its correct and tantalizing action. And, it's extremely difficult to set the hook properly when the tip collapses as you attempt to drive the point through tough flesh.

Ideal action rods, whether they are spinning, fly or plug casting, should be medium action; action that comes well down into the rod, giving you some flexibility on the cast, but a smooth fighting curve when you battle the fish after the strike. Spinning reels for flats fishing don't have to be expensive, but they must have two important characteristics—a good roller and drag. If either of these features is missing

160

you'll lose the permit, bonefish, and any other fast-running fishes, especially if you prefer to use lighter lines.

You can check rollers in stores for possible acceptance. Take a 6-inch piece of monofilament and work it across the roller. It should roll instantly as you apply pressure and move the line back and forth. If it doesn't, reject that reel.

A spinning reel that has a roller that will continue to roll under hard use will have an insert, or bushing, between the shaft and the roller. It's a simple matter to remove the roller, or have the tackle dealer do it, and see that it does have that vital bushing. Also, never grease a roller for fishing—grease is too stiff—instead use light oil.

Carbide rollers are not good for saltwater use, either. Carbide is a super-hard metal, perfectly fine for fresh water, but salt water reacts with carbide and under hard use, even if carefully cleaned between trips, will cause the roller to become rough—and ruin a good spinning line that travels over it.

The drag is a little hard to check in a store. But look at the exploded drawing of the drag that comes in the box with the reel. If the drawing does not show several washers in use, then don't buy the reel. Also, at least one or two of the metal washers should have projections on them, so they lock in the cavity where the washers lie, preventing them from spinning under use.

Most important of all, the drag washers should be alternately hard and soft materials. If your drag has a hard material rubbing on another hard material, the drag will heat up under a fast run from a fish and probably cause you to lose it through a broken line.

Drags should be super smooth. You can easily check this by running the spinning line through the guides, then have a youngster run away from you with the line end as the drag is adjusted to what you feel is light, fighting pressure. If the tip dives and waves like a conductor's baton, that means the drag is releasing line in lurches—something that breaks lines quickly in battle.

If you have already bought a reel that produces this, you can often smooth it up by attaching the line to a bicycle seat, then have your youngster drive off a 100 yards rather fast, with the drag set fairly light, about 1 pound of running drag. If the washers have high spots that cause the lurching, the pull from the bicycle will generally smooth them up for you. Sometimes you can substitute washers made from another

Two all-time favorite bonefish lures—left, Popeye jig by Nicklelure; and Phillips Wiggle Jig.

Baby tarpon live among the mangroves along the flats. Here, Charley Wells, Greenbelt, Maryland, unhooks one he will release.

reel (maybe you will have to cut and trim a little to get them to fit) that will make a much-improved drag.

Fly reels for flats fishing should have a plain but adequate drag. Much of the pressure used as drag when fighting a fish on a fly reel comes when the angler presses his fingers against the inside edge of the spool flange, increasing or decreasing pressure as he sees fit.

Lures for fishing the flats are relatively simple. Bucktails, commonly called jigs, will take most species. Often, when the flats are very shallow, as with permit and bonefish, the jigs will be shaped flat, with the hook riding upright. The Phillips Wiggle Jig and Nicklelure's Popeye Jig are favored—the latter has accounted for more permit than perhaps any artificial lure. The Phillips is deadly on bonefish, with a track record extending back many years. Such jigs can be allowed to drop right to the bottom. With the hooks upright, they will rarely tangle in the flat's debris.

Other jigs are effective on many inshore species from ladyfish and snapper to mackerel and jack crevalle. The lima bean-shaped jig weighing from $\frac{3}{16}$- to $\frac{1}{2}$-ounce is a universal jig for taking many species of inshore fishes and should be carried in every flats fisherman's tackle box.

A new jig, which I feel is superior to any of the older styles, is the plastic-tipped jig. This lure has a standard type jig head, but various colors of plastic tails are slipped over the hook. Vic Dunaway, Florida's best-known outdoor writer, and I made a movie a few seasons ago on fishing in Florida Bay. Using only this type of jig we managed to catch 15 different species of fish from pompano to kingfish—all fooled by the plastic-tail lure. Color of the plastic does not seem to be too important most of the time. I favor green, white, and bright orange. Yet, I have consistently had great catches on black, purple, blue, and many other colors.

The list of fishes that will hit these plastic-tail lures is amazing: bonefish, bluefish, striped bass, snappers, groupers, kingfish, jack crevalle, cobia, tarpon, and trout. The new style of this lure has a tail molded in waves, so that as the lure is moved through the water the tail wigwags, much as the tail would on a swimming eel. It's deadly.

Vic and I have caught many sea trout, and we both feel that plastic-tipped lures are better than live shrimp. Every flats fisherman should have a few of these lures in his box. Sizes for most fishing are $\frac{3}{8}$- to $\frac{1}{2}$-ounce and in an assortment of colors.

Every inshore fisherman I know who has much experience has learned about the Mirrolure, and its durability and appeal to fish. The 52M is a standard lure, perhaps the finest choice for a flats-fishing plug. The Sea Bee is another superb lure, appearing to be a silvery minnow of the Rapala style, but made from super-tough plastic. I have caught as many as 14 barracudas on one of these lures without the lure falling apart—a testimony to its toughness. Both the 52 M Mirrolure and the Sea Bee are deadly on any flats fishes that feed on minnows: snook, sharks, jack crevalle, barracuda and others.

One barracuda lure stands above all others, it's the tube lure. Northern coastal fishermen, trolling for bluefish and striped bass, have for years been taking both species on the tube lure. It is simply a 12-inch length of surgical tubing with a hook or two in the lure. With a slight

Kids and 'cudas go well together. Eager to catch a fish, the boy (Larry Kreh) can cast to fish that are just as eager to strike.

Captain Tate Berry, Key West, lifts aboard a barracuda to be unhooked and released.

adaptation to how it is used, the tube lure is the most deadly spinning and plug-casting lure you can get for barracuda. The tube is cast as far as possible to one side of the barracuda, then, before the lure strikes the water, the angler begins reeling as fast as he can.

The tube skips across the surface, bouncing and jumping, exactly like a needlefish escaping. The 'cuda that sees this just can't resist it. A fly, made from Fish Hair, a trade name for light, silky synthetic fibers, is almost as deadly as the tube lure. The fly, 10 to 12 inches long, made of no more than 30 or 40 strands of the material, is cast to one side of a barracuda and retrieved slowly back. They can't resist it.

The angler can always find specific lures for special flats situations, but if he uses the above casting lures and an assortment of the conventional flies, plus the newer barracuda fly just mentioned, he will be able to operate rather well on the flats.

Much of flats fishing is looking, or hunting, then trying to catch the quarry. This combination of hunting and fishing is considered by many anglers as the very best of fishing thrills.

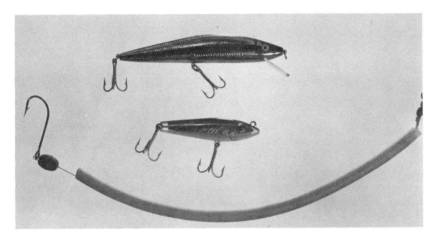

Three good basic lures for flats fishing . . . top—Sea Bee; middle—Mirro-lure 52 M; and bottom—tube lure for barracudas.

Three good basic jigs for flats fishing—top is two sizes of the lima bean style jig, lower is a jig head (Salty Dog) with a plastic tail.

Charles F. Waterman with an 8-pound brown trout that took a late fall streamer.

166

A Look at Western Trout

CHARLES F. WATERMAN

A long time ago a well-traveled angler told me the West was a land of big rivers, fast water and large stupid trout.

There still are some naive trout in the West and the big fast rivers are there for sure, but my friend oversimplified things. The West has your kind of trout fishing, whatever it is, and any classic angler who cares to bring his entomology from England or Pennsylvania will find his match in Western fishermen and Western waters. For that matter, a fly man can bring the same rod he uses for striped bass or Atlantic salmon and find room to use it.

But there's no purpose in extolling the West or its trout. People have been doing that since Lewis and Clark wrote the first report. I'll just try to explain some of the things a visiting angler might not have thought of.

There is the business of the high-mountain snow pack which provides water for a large share of the West's trout streams. Through the winter you watch the weather page but you know much of the runoff depends upon what happens in spring. The heavier the snow pack the more high water you can expect around the beginning of fishing season, but just when the water will come down depends upon spring temperatures.

There's some winter fishing, even at the foot of the most northern Rockies, but you don't hear much about it. Long trips can't be planned

Gently flowing spring creeks provide top trout fishing, but they're also the most difficult waters to fish in the West. This is Armstrong's Creek near Livingston, Montana.

around it because cold weather can move in overnight and your line will freeze in the air. Only a part of the rivers have legal winter fishing.

There are really two summer fishing seasons in the snow-fed rivers each year. Before the hibernating marmots even begin to yawn in their dens on the rocky slopes, the valleys have warmed up, the ice gradually disappears and the water can be clear in the big rivers. That period often ends abruptly when a hot sun strikes the peaks for several days in succession and the canyons roar with brown water and bouncing driftwood. This may last for a long while before a final clear-up that will continue on into the fall except for muddy interludes caused by summer rains.

Flood is a part of the stream ecology but it can upset an early season trip unless your plans are flexible. In most areas vulnerable to sudden runoff, there are small streams beginning at low levels and frequently clear while the big rivers are booming. At any rate, the frequent visitor to Western streams needs ready sources of information about water conditions and he does much of his fishing by telephone.

The first June we went to Montana we found the Yellowstone the color of creamed coffee and glumly presented ourselves at Dan Bailey's Fly Shop in Livingston to learn what we should do. There was no problem at all, we learned. We got a list of streams that were clear and full of trout. Fact is, we never did get back to the Yellowstone that time.

Don't put all of your eggs in one basket. When dealing with Western fishing, think in terms of areas and central headquarters rather than of a single creek or river. Things change from year to year, but there's nearly always good fishing somewhere in a river system once the general season opens.

There are two basic fly-fishing outfits for the West—one for the big streamers in big rivers and one for dry flies and nymphs. The big rod comes close to what a black-bass fisherman would use for bugs; the lighter one can be anything he'd use for small stream fishing anywhere. Twenty-five years ago Syl MacDowell wrote of tourist fishermen standing awed on the bank of a plunging Western torrent and pining for the quiet brooks of their Eastern home. MacDowell said he'd steered the lost souls to smaller water and they were happy. I've seen such things happen many times since then. If you don't see what you want, ask for it. If you don't like big water, you can leave your big rod at home and stay busy anyway.

But let's discuss the heavy outfit. Frankly, it's been getting huskier right along. It's been about 20 years since the big streamer business really got started and today you'll find earnest people fishing for brown trout with the same rods they'd use for striped bass or tarpon. It isn't that they need all that power for the fish, but they do need it for the big streamers and giant Woolly Worms they try to span the big rivers with each fall. It's in the fall that the big stuff crowds other tackle aside.

First they put big streamers on their double-tapered lines and found something was lacking. Then they got forward-tapered lines and distance improved. They went to rods that took No. 8 lines (that was called GBF in those days) and things worked better. But all that time the steelhead anglers along the Pacific Coast were working up outfits with sinking heads and monofilament running line that carried steelhead flies clear across the heavy current and let them bump along the bottom. The steelhead outfits moved inland 10 years ago and caught larger fish. In the fall of 1974 there were top anglers throwing with No. 10 rods and sinking heads for big browns and rainbows. The same people carried little rods in their cars to be used on the spring creeks, the fast mountain brooks, and with dry flies in the big rivers' side channels.

Fly selection for the spring creeks of the valleys can become complicated, for it's a matter of matching hatches, but there are hundreds of miles of water where good-size dries of only a few patterns will do well, especially in summer. Imitation 'hoppers are excellent and the Royal Wulff in 12 or 14 is a favorite. Any bushy fly that's highly visible and a good floater will work in the swift, broken water of steep rocky streams, and while fly selection may be unimportant there must be some careful casting. It is that kind of fishing, however, that has given the Western trout a reputation for simplicity. If you feel geography makes for duplicity, try some of the spring creeks.

"Spring creek" is a loose term and generally refers to meadow streams, not too swift, and with considerable vegetation. In some such creeks there are regular hatches of very small mayflies all summer and fall. There are anglers who speak freely of No. 22 and even No. 24 flies used on such streams. Something a little larger will usually work but you'll frequently need No. 16 or smaller. If I had to use a single dry fly for all spring creeks of the West I'd probably choose a No. 18 Light Cahill, but it's simply because I got started with it and any number of similar ties would probably be just as good. Of course there are times when something very different is called for, but that's a start and is near enough in a surprisingly large percentage of the situations. I've caught many fish with it when the hatch was quite different.

There are some larger-than-life hatches on the big waters, the most publicized being the salmon fly, actually a big stone fly that appears in early summer on many Western rivers. The hatch works upstream, ending in the high mountains, and there are some years when it occurs while most of the fishing water is muddy. It's difficult to count on being present when the best of it occurs, but it is one situation in which the larger big-river trout consistently rise to large dry flies. Here again, the answer is constant communication with someone on the scene and I'd certainly plan no short vacation aimed solely at the salmon flies.

I've struck two of those hatches, one on the Madison River of western Montana and one later in the year after it had moved up the Yellowstone into Yellowstone National Park. Up there the fish were cutthroats instead of the browns and rainbows that made up the bulk of the catch lower down. The artificials used to imitate the stone flies are big, bushy and more than 1 inch long, regardless of the hook size, and the squirrel tail Sofa Pillow is one of the best, riding high along with the froth of a boiling current.

It's an experience that stays with you. You lean against the heavy water with the enormous naturals drifting past out of control and you push your big fly well out over the main flow. Two-pound trout can be

Trout of this size are frequently taken on dry flies during Western salmon fly hatches.

Left to right: Muddler, Spruce Fly, and Spuddler. All typical of the very large streamers used for fall fishing in the West.

routine and flashes of much broader fish under your imitation will cause you to squeeze the cork grip until your fingers ache. It is one of the most spectacular of the Western trout programs. Mid-June might be as good a bet as any period, but the hatch varies with the river.

It is in fall that the streamer fishermen wear thermal underwear, shiver and cast to the biggest fish of all. The big streamers often imitate the "bullhead" or caddis and are generally worked close to the bottom. The Muddler Minnow and its endless variations in color and materials are about as good as any. The Spruce Fly, a good streamer itself, is combined with the Muddler to produce the "Spuddler," and enthusiastic tyers come up with all sorts of creations. The bigger streamers do take the bigger fish within reason.

172

I think the burr-headed relatives of the Muddler may have an edge most of the time, but any good streamer may work and some of the best fish I've taken have been on variations of the Silver Doctor. This is the time of year when brown trout, if not actually spawning, are in preparation for it, and it's the best time if you want fish of 3 pounds or more. Most fall fishing begins in early September, but unseasonably hot weather can postpone it. In the northern Rockies the streamer fishing can last well into November but a trip planned after mid-October is likely to run afoul of really cold weather, slush, ice and snow.

If I must take something from the big-streamer fishing it is this: To catch those fall fish you should be equipped with the same tackle that works on much larger fish such as Atlantic salmon or steelhead. So it adds up to pretty heavy gear for 2- or 3-pound trout.

Spinning or light plugging gear will get its best results in fall and the spoons can be pretty big. Keep them close to the bottom.

Wading the swift, rocky streams is not to be taken lightly. Twenty years ago nearly all Western fly fishermen used felt soles and they are perfect for small valley waters, but wading is one of the bugaboos of the Western trout guide.

"If I can keep them upright I can find fish for them," one veteran says. "But half of my work is trying to keep my clients dry."

All sorts of cleats and spikes are used in the big, fast rivers, usually of aluminum or soft steel, and it is no department in which to pinch pennies. Western waders are expensive and a sure footing staves off exhaustion at least, if not dangerous falls. It isn't so much a matter of being drowned as a matter of being soaked and bruised. The regulars tend to spend more for waders and cleats than they do for tackle.

After several years of teetering in Wyoming, Montana and Idaho rivers, I journeyed to British Columbia's Kispiox for steelhead. The Kispiox, I was told, was wild and swift and I worried about my footing, but compared to the Madison or Yellowstone the Kispiox was easy walking. I must emphasize this wading business. It has made fishing almost impossible for some tourists, generally because they lacked proper equipment.

Use of a boat on the Western waters is so often tied in with smashing haystacks in rivers of no return that many serious anglers discount it as a simple, efficient method of getting to pools that see few fishermen. The boat becomes important in view of access problems as ranchers

The McKenzie boat is widely used by Western fishing guides. High stern works well as the boat goes downstream in swift current.

A pod of fly-casters use floating bubbles in the cold water of Henry's Lake, Idaho. Such outfits cause less disturbance than boats but provide very slow transportation.

A small float boat is lined down a swift side channel of the Yellowstone. Boatman is guide Ray Hurley, who will work the channel's mouth before continuing downstream.

and farmers resist the inroads of the thousands of tourists. Anyone who travels extensively by automobile or camper will do well to consider a craft of his own.

But before you launch your own boat consider the float-fishing guide, a fellow who has become more and more important in Western fishing. It's true that guide boats will take you to fishing spots along the really dangerous rivers where there's no other way to go, but many of them

175

operate on less breathtaking streams. These operators will learn their miles of water, will know where the best pools are, will know what's wadable, even for a stumbling neophyte, and will enable a caster to cover more good water in a day than he could cover in a week on foot. Some of the casting, especially for spinfishermen, can be done from the boat itself. But the most efficient method on most rivers is to go from pool to pool and wade in the good places. Some of the willow-lined rivers are exceptions and you stay in the boat.

Until recent years there was a long period when nearly all guides on moderately fast rivers used rubber boats or life rafts. Now there is a trend toward the aluminum johnboat, generally about 14 feet, on the quieter rivers and toward the dorylike McKenzie boat where there is considerable white water.

The rubber doughnut lost favor with guides because it was not maneuverable. The johnboat is light enough to be carried atop a car or truck and, although its slightly uptilted square ends are not exactly the ideal for fast water, it is much easier to row in the wind. One of the best compromises between the two is the keeled inflated boat shaped with a sharp bow, intended for use with the larger outboards. It has extra safety plus considerable maneuverability with oars. It is an excellent, although expensive, choice for someone who takes his own boat. The McKenzie boat, high at both ends, is generally too heavy for cartopping and guides use them with trailers.

Canoes are seldom used by Western trout guides since they operate under an entirely different principle. A canoe being used with a paddle must be driven faster than the current for steerage and that makes for difficult fishing. The inflated boats, the johnboats, the McKenzies and the assorted skiffs are rowed against the current as they drift downward and achieve their steerage while being slowed down. Fine for fishing. The typical johnboat or McKenzie takes a guide and two fishermen. Some Westerners, using spinning tackle for the most part, employ large life rafts in picnic style—but that's not the most efficient fishing rig.

Float fishing is a solution in areas where owners of the riverbanks will not allow fishing from shore. The law varies in Western states, but most waters that are classified as navigable may be fished as long as the fisherman doesn't get out on dry land. Wyoming has had rancher-fisherman wars and the laws there are less tolerant. In much Wyoming fishing, you have to stay in the boat unless you have permission from landowners. In some states the fisherman is entitled to use the river bottoms if he stays inside the normal high-water line and doesn't cross inhospitable ranch land to get there.

Twenty years ago a visit to almost any Western sporting goods store, or even to a service station, was likely to net an invitation to fish somebody's private water—but in areas where tourism has boomed the ranchers' welcome mat has worn thin. Usually it is hunting that has brought animosity, but the status of fishermen can change. For example, when housewives staged a meat strike some time back, many Colorado ranchers took their frustrations out on the sportsmen and access became impossible in large sections.

Although most of the large rivers remain accessible and state access areas are becoming more plentiful, some of the most rare and valuable meadow streams are being leased by private individuals and groups. Others are operated with daily fishing fees. The costs are skyrocketing. About $10 to $15 per rod per day is fairly representative. Most fishing resorts and guest ranches have their own water, available only to guests. The larger outfits often have stocked ponds for those who don't demand wild trout.

Fly fishing a small Western river for rainbows. A trout here heads for the protection of a midstream rock.

Hiking fishermen escape crowds and find waters where trout are plentiful.

Pack trips for high country trout are often on National Forest land, and although they may not get you to the largest trout they are almost certain to get you where the fish are plentiful. The full-scale horse packing expedition has an appeal of its own but anyone willing to climb a bit with a pack and a rod can generally reach sophisticated fish. Not long ago I hiked for only 3 hours with a promise of golden trout in a mountain lake. It was hard to believe the treasured goldens were so near to a parking place, but before I could string my rod I saw the flashes of flame under natural insects and my second cast brought a 10-incher with a rush. Goldens, originally residents of only a small sector of California high country, have been planted in many high lakes and streams.

A Look at Western Trout

Yellowstone Park is becoming America's best place for quality trout angling. The meat fishing of "Fishing Bridge" is long gone under new policies and last summer I stood in a virtually unknown Yellowstone stream and had ¼-mile of excellent dry fly water to myself. There were cutthroats, browns, and rainbows, and 2-pounders were not unusual. It was catch-and-release water, not calculated to appeal to the multitudes. Some famous park streams like the Firehole are now less crowded, a result of regulations aimed at quality angling instead of fish fries.

In one creek, Soda Butte, I caught good cutthroats in fast water and then found them rising to tiny insects in a meadow slough nearby. Do it right and you'd take a good fish, but it was the kind of hands-and-knees delicacy generally associated with hard-worked Eastern brooks.

No one who fishes the West has covered it all and the choice spots of one trout hunter might be disappointing to another, simply a matter of many kinds of trout fishing for many kinds of trout fishermen. Let's just say I'm going to mention some good places for headquarters. All of these spots are very near to a variety of water including large and small streams.

Saratoga, Wyoming, will put you on the North Platte and the En-

Delicate fly fishing in a small creek of Yellowstone National Park. Fish here are cutthroats.

campment and some of the best dry-fly fishing in the country for rainbow and brown trout. When I first visited the Platte more than 20 years ago we went there from Denver, followed meticulous instructions given by Fred DeBell, the rod maker, and hiked across sagebrush hills to the river. It was low water in early fall and the pools were sluggish.

With an antelope buck watching from a nearby bluff, I hooked something heavy, floundered a bit on slippery rocks, and landed a brown of more than 4 pounds, the biggest wild trout I'd ever seen. I clutched it and photographed it until I doubted that it should be released and then we walked back to the car as dusk came on. As I prepared to dress my fish, an operation postponed until the last minute, a sheepherder came by and I gave it to him. His eyes got big, he muttered thanks and I like to think he was feeling for firewood with his feet as he hurried toward his camp, the trout held well out in front.

There are small streams near Saratoga, most of them on private property, and some of the fishing is pretty technical, but there is also some good float water for somewhat coarser methods.

Lander, Wyoming, is another good spot. There is the Wind River above and Boysen Reservoir below and the smaller creeks can be found if you enquire.

At Pinedale, you'll be near to the famous Green River, noted for big fish but with touchy regulations about float activity. There are the Boulder, New Fork, East River and some fine lakes. There is Duck Creek with the big browns that insist on delicate operations.

Colorado suffers from enormous tourist centers and a booming population on the eastern slope, but Glenwood Springs is a fine location. There is the Frying Pan where I've been proud of myself and also humiliated by educated fish. There is the Eagle River, the Colorado, the Roaring Fork and the Crystal. And Colorado's high country begins in almost any direction if deep, cold lakes are your passion.

Farther south at Durango or Pagosa Springs, there is fine fishing, less publicized than some of that farther north. There is the San Juan, the Los Pinos, the Piedra, the Animas, the Conejos and the Rio Grande. Forty years ago an elderly man with a broken bamboo fly rod spliced with twine tried to show me how to catch Rio Grande trout with nameless flies he'd tied himself. He caught the fish and I watched. We were alone on the river then and although you'd probably have company now, the fish are still there.

A fine brown trout from Montana's Beaverhead River.

Use Ketchum, Idaho, as a jumping-off place and there is famous Silver Creek where Ray Donnersberger gave me a lesson with nymphs on a barely flowing slough. There are Wood River and Little Wood River. There is limestone water for delicate flies. The Snake River and its tributaries seem reluctant to leave Idaho and, although they are better publicized for steelhead, there are stay-at-home trout over much of the state.

181

This big, leaping trout took a small nymph in a quiet Montana slough.

We must consider the Yellowstone Park area in more than one segment. To the north of the park itself are the Madison and Yellowstone, most famous of all, and each has its list of tributaries, some of them carrying gullible little fish in splashy snow-fed creeks, and some of them carrying big, educated veterans in meadow brooks.

In the past 15 years, I've missed only one season at Livingston,

182

Montana, not exactly a resort town but a sort of gathering place for fishermen from all over the world, some of them bent on leaning into the Yellowstone itself and some of them preferring the little creeks, some of which are pay-as-you-go these days. Undoubtedly there are other headquarters just as good but it's within an hour's drive of Yellowstone Park, not too far south of the Missouri and within casting distance of some big trout and some good guides.

Over on the Madison, Ennis has its own group of regulars. West Yellowstone has a good share of neon signs and the tourists can be thick and noisy in season, but it just may be America's most important trout fishing center. It's a headquarters for guides and it has fine tackle shops—and the airport handles jet planes. You could be completely equipped there in a matter of minutes. Some of the guest ranches like Parade Rest cater to fishermen and you can get fishing information almost anywhere.

Those spots are not necessarily the best but they are very good. The best wild trout fishing of the coastal states is now in the high country for the most part. The steelhead and salmon rivers of Washington and Oregon get more attention than their resident trout.

Now nobody is likely to say there are undiscovered trout waters in the West, but there certainly are undeveloped areas. And there's a lot of good trout fishing that a lot of good trout fishermen are keeping very, very quiet. Look for yourself.

Sixteen-pound Group "B" steelhead is hefted by Jim Bates on Snake River below Clarkston. Brad O'Connor photo.

184

Chasing the Steelhead

EMMIT GLANZ

It is said that in California's Trinity River Valley, when the word goes out on a fall day that "steelies are in," barber shops close in mid-haircut, cars are left on grease racks and soup congeals.

The cause of all this is a rambunctious rainbow trout called *Salmo gairdneri,* or more commonly, steelhead. There is considerable speculation regarding the origin of the term, and even whether it applies to the fishermen or the fish. But tradition holds that the metallic, blue-steel appearance of the fish's back gave rise to the name. More colorful nomenclature is applied from time to time by bug-eyed anglers left staring at a hole in the water beyond a suddenly lifeless rod tip.

Spawned in freshwater streams from Alaska to California, steelheads become footloose after a couple of years and head for the Pacific Ocean. Anywhere from 1½ to four years later, depending upon their degree of wanderlust and appetite, they return to their natal rivers to spawn. Amply nourished in the pastures of the sea, mature fish weigh from 2 to more than 30 pounds.

Steelhead are rarely caught in salt water, even by long liners and other commercial fishermen who ply the north Pacific. Unlike salmon, steelhead are solitary wanderers, ranging far beyond the continental shelf, northward to arctic waters and southward until surface temperatures reach 59 degrees.

This independent spirit, overcome temporarily by the spawning impulse and unerringly directed to the natal stream, reasserts itself immediately upon encountering an object placed in the water by a hopeful angler.

Be it hardware, plastic, or hackled, the steelhead's reaction will range from utter disdain through casual interest to savage assault. If hooked, it will almost invariably become violent. Steelhead jump higher, run farther, sulk longer, and pull harder than any freshwater fish I have encountered, with the possible exception of Atlantic salmon.

Steelhead top the gamefish list in Alaska and British Columbia. Closer to home, they are native to four states: California, Oregon, Washington and Idaho. Virtually every coastal stream from California's Santa Ynez River northward hosts the seagoing rainbow, but in relatively meager numbers south of the Sacramento River.

There are two major seasonal strains of steelhead—winter run and summer run, with the former predominating. Some larger streams like the Klamath, Columbia and Skagit, however, hold good numbers of fish all year.

All rainbows, including the steelhead, spawn in early spring. The summer-run and early fall fish come in from the ocean early and remain in fresh water until spawning time. Usually, these are the fish that have the farthest to go. Unlike the Pacific salmon, steelhead do not always die after spawning, and many return several times to the conjugal gravel beds.

Hatchery production has greatly enhanced the steelhead population in many of the major steelhead streams. Millions of steelhead smolts are reared to migratory size in these ichthyologic greenhouses in half the time nature takes, and sent seaward a year after they emerge from the egg. Some of the most productive steelhead waters would yield sparsely at best without them.

The jury is still out on whether steelies feed after reentering fresh water on the spawning run. Most authorities hold that they do not, although many fish, particularly summer runs, exhibit predatory characteristics. Two things are certain: The steelhead is catholic in its response to bait or lure, and arcane in its reasons why.

At one time or another, steelhead will bite anything any other trout will. Worms, single or cluster eggs, herring, smelt, marshmallows and Velveeta cheese are fair game. So are shrimp, clams, mussels, grasshoppers, and fat-bodied moths. All manner of hardware and a variety of fly patterns will also get the job done, as will fluorescent yarn and an assortment of plastic balls and bobbers.

Aside from the possible motivation of hunger, steelhead may be prompted to strike by irritability, self-preservation or simple curiosity. Steelheader patriarch Enos Bradner's stock reply to the question of why the fish mouth some of these objects is, "Because they don't have any fingers."

Whatever the reason, these prime gamefish can be, and are, taken on all the above lures, enticements, and more. But for all intents and purposes, some produce more consistently than others, though the basic presentation is the same.

The standard steelhead bait is roe—salmon or steelhead eggs prepared and presented in as natural a manner as possible. In low clear water, single eggs or small clusters are used on hooks as small as No. 8. In heavier water, as is usually encountered in winter and spring months, larger clusters are used on No. 2, 1, or 1/0 hooks.

Fresh eggs are best, but have three significant drawbacks: they are difficult to come by, messy to handle, and hard to keep on the hook. Boraxed eggs are also not easy to come by, but they are much easier to handle, stay on the hook better, and keep longer. The egg skein is first dried and toughened by soaking in a 3-to-1 water-and-borax solution for an hour or so, or by rolling in powdered borax, wrapping in absorbent towels, and placing in the refrigerator for a day. If your wife permits you to do this, you have married well.

The skein is then split lengthwise, cut into thumbnail-size clusters with an old scissors, and rolled or shaken in powdered borax. Clusters may be put up in old margarine or frozen food containers, topped off with a layer of powdered borax, and frozen for later use.

At streamside, the angler carries the egg clusters in a bait box clipped to his belt. Single eggs are impaled singly or several on the hook, and clusters are affixed with an "egg loop." When the hook is tied, the line is snugged around the shank below the eye and then slid down to where the hook begins to bend. The line below the hook eye can then be pulled out to form a loop, which is tightened around the egg cluster to hold it in place.

Many veteran anglers tie a bit of fluorescent yarn to the loop. It helps to pull the loop open, tends to catch in a steelhead's teeth, and adds an extra attractor at the end of your line. Other baits are rigged much the same as for any trout . . . to present them as attractively and as realistically as possible.

Plastic or Styrofoam bobbers in sundry shapes, sizes and colors are often used in lieu of egg clusters. These bobbers have a hole in the center and are slid down the leader atop the hook eye. Some, like the Okie Drifter, are shaped to resemble an egg cluster. Others are round or pear-shaped and some have "wings" which make them revolve in the current.

Most popular shades are red, pink, and orange, although every color of the rainbow will produce under the right conditions. Generally speaking, the clearer the water the smaller the bobber and paler the color. In heavy water, larger and more garish bobbers are often used in combination with yarn, spinners, or roe.

Yarn flies are also effective. Fluorescent red, pink, orange, and green are preferred colors, singly or in combination. Three separate strands of yarn are tied to the egg loop or above the hook eye, fluffed with a comb or stiff brush, and trimmed even with the bend of the hook.

Wobbling spoons 1 to 3 inches long—striped, dotted or in solid bright fluorescent hues, or in nickel, bronze or copper—are favored by hardware fishermen. Weighted spinners of the Mepps or Mounti type, in nickel, brass or copper, are preferred in Size 4 or 5.

Diving plugs are often used by boat fishermen. The Hotshot is so effective that periodic attempts have been made to have it banned. Tad Pollys, Flatfish, and the new Lazy Ike Jawbreaker also get the job done. A number of metallic colors are effective, with silver or chrome among the best.

Flies used for steelhead are generally large and tied wet, with fairly sparse hackle and wings. Fly fishermen are particular, and most have their tried and true patterns. Some of the more widely used patterns are the Skunk, Thor, Royal Coachman, Purple Peril, Skykomish Sunrise, and Muddler Minnow. Some dry fly fishing is done for summer steelhead with patterns like the Wulff and Bucktail Caddis.

Steelhead enter their stream with one objective in mind—to reach the spawning grounds. To this end they leap falls, shoot rapids, belly through shallows and fight anything that stands in their way. But, like all crea-

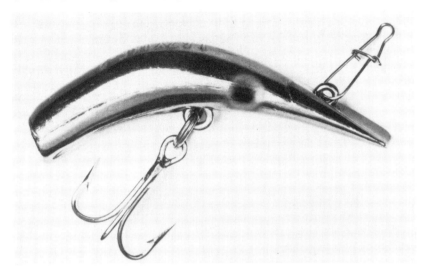

"Jawbreaker" by Lazy Ike was developed after years of experimentation by some of Oregon and Washington's top steelhead guides.

tures, their energy is finite. Instinctively, they seek the upstream route that is easiest to negotiate and offers the best cover.

The fisherman attempts to intercept his fish in its upstream path or tempt it in its resting place. To do this, it is necessary to "read the water." With practice, an angler can develop considerable facility at this.

Steelhead hold behind, in front of, or alongside rocks or other obstructions in the current, beneath overhanging brush or logs, and beside ledges. They frequent deep pockets or slots, and either end of a pool. They shun eddies and quiet backwaters, preferring instead to lie just off the main current, in water 3 to 8 feet deep, where they can hold position with a minimum of effort, but escape to the main current if danger threatens.

Once the steelheader determines where to fish, he has a choice of two basic methods—plunking or drifting. Personal inclination and water conditions will determine his choice.

The plunker casts into a likely looking hole, places his rod in a holder and waits for a fish to come along. The drifter goes after his quarry, seeking out runs, slots and pockets, and allowing the current to "drift" his offering through.

Either way, the steelhead must be pursued on or near the bottom. Summer steelhead will rise to a fly, and winter fish occasionally chase a lure to the surface. But 99½ percent of the time, if your terminal gear is not within a few inches of the bottom, it may as well be in your tackle box.

Plunking is most effective in high, dirty water or in deep holes where the current flows slowly. It requires a heavy-duty rod and reel, with line of 20-pound-test or better. Sinkers must either be heavy enough or shaped so they will stay in place.

The sinker is hung 15 to 20 inches below a three-way swivel, with a 2- to 3-foot leader trailing off above it. Large winged bobbers like the Spin-N-Glo are a favorite with plunkers, as are plugs and unweighted spinners.

But most steelheaders are drifters. Drift fishermen cover more water and get more exercise than plunkers do. And the next slot, pocket or run just might hold the fish that makes the whole day worthwhile. Steelhead drift fishermen use either spinning or conventional bait-casting gear, with the latter perhaps the more efficient and the former easier to use. The important thing is to acquire a good quality, balanced outfit. A niggardly rib is a good investment as long as you do not hook a fish. Any steelhead worth his gill covers will turn a cheap outfit into a handful of junk in 10 seconds flat.

The rod should be 8 to 9 feet long, with a light tip, sturdy butt section and two-handed cork grip. The reel should be substantial with a large-capacity spool. All components of both—line guides, reel seat, drag system, spool, gears—should be first-rate. Monofilament line should be soft enough to lay out well but hard enough to resist fraying on rocks and snags. Depending upon water conditions and how long you like to play your fish, optimum line strength will be from 8- to 15-pound-test.

A "pencil" lead is attached to the terminal end of the line. Hollow lead can be pinched onto a dropper line; solid lead is inserted into a short length of rubber surgical tubing slid up the line or attached to a swivel. If the lead hangs up, it will pull free and save the other terminal gear. A 17- to 20-inch leader, with eggs, bobber, yarn or fly on the business end, completes the rig. Normally the leader will be lighter than the main line, to save line in event of a snag.

The drifter casts at about 45 degrees upstream from where he stands. If the cast is made correctly and the sinker is the proper weight, it will bounce along the bottom. The line should remain as taut as possible, for steelhead strike this type of offering gently and a slack or bellied line minimizes your chance to feel it, or to set the hook if you do. The sinker will bang and bump along the bottom, encountering rocks, vegetation, and a variety of objects along the way. Each time, your rod tip will jerk. So how do you feel a fish?

The best procedure is, if there is any doubt, set the hook—hard! You're bound to lose gear that way, but if anything feels strange or out of the ordinary, set the hook. After a time, you'll know which is a fish and which is the river bottom.

Spoons and weighted spinners are cast straight across or very slightly upstream and allowed to sink as the current carries them downstream in an arc through the drift. Plugs are usually fished from a boat, as their progress must be slowed so the pressure of the current imparts action and inclines them toward the bottom.

Steelhead usually strike spoons, spinners and plugs with authority. No mouthing the bait or gentle tugs—the fish is either on or off! For this reason, exasperated neophytes often forsake egg-and-bobber drifting for hardware. If they make this a permanent practice, however, they

Fly fisherman connects with summer-run steelhead on Oregon's renowned Deschutes River. Don Schomberg photo.

limit their fish-taking potential. Steelhead are difficult fish to catch, and versatility shortens the odds against the angler.

Fly fishing is gaining in popularity for both winter-run and summer-run steelhead. In winter, flies are drifted wet in the same manner as eggs, bobbers or yarn. In summer, they are used with floating line or floating line with a sinking tip.

Summer-run streams like Washington's Klickitat and Oregon's famed Deschutes River are prime fly-fishing waters. A growing number of specialty shops in Portland, Seattle, and other major Pacific Northwest cities cater to fishermen who believe the ultimate angling thrill is taking a steelhead on a fly.

Any attempt to catalog Northwest steelhead waters would require a book in itself. I'll list the major streams and add some detail on the top producers, beginning in California and working north through Oregon, Washington and Idaho.

CALIFORNIA

MAJOR STEELHEAD STREAMS

Albion River	Gualala River	Salmon River
American River	Klamath River	San Lorenzo River
Battle Creek	Mad River	Scott River
Big River	Mattole River	Shasta River
Big Sur River	Mill Creek	Smith River
Butte Creek	Napa River	Ten Mile River
Carmel River	Navarro River	Trinity River
Deer Creek	Noyo River	Van Duzen River
Eel River	Papermill Creek	Yuba River
Feather River	Russian River	
Garcia River	Sacramento River	

TOP PRODUCERS

American River: Tributary of Sacramento River. "Half-pounders" (small steelhead) start showing in September, with bigger fish November through March. Bank fishing most of length, with boats used near mouth. Nightcrawlers effective early in season, with yarn "glo bugs" and roe best December through March. Lures productive anytime. Flies produce when river is low and clear.

192

CHASING THE STEELHEAD

    Eel River: Coastal. Half-pounders show below Van Duzen River in late summer, larger fish in main river and forks fall and winter. Good fishing in flurries when river not muddy. Middle Fork has summer steelhead. Bank fishing most of length, with boats near mouth.

    Feather River: Sacramento River tributary. September until early spring. Upper river fished from bank, lower stretches boatable. Fresh roe and lures best, with some fly fishing below Oroville Dam.

    Klamath River: Coastal. Half-pounders to mid-size fish in river all year. Larger fish November to February. Bank and boat fishermen jam mouth and lagoon August and September. Boat access only from Highway 101 up-

Klamath River guide Jim Roads smiles as he views catch of steelhead. Shasta-Cascade Wonderland Association photo.

Bright "steelie" from Battle Creek, a tributary of California's Sacramento River. Shasta-Cascade Wonderland Association photo.

stream to Johnson's Bank and/or boat fishing from there up. Best spots at tributary mouths. Bait, lures, plugs, flies all produce.

Russian River: Coastal. November through February, but may be delayed if rains are late. Fishing in flurries when water conditions permit. Accessible most of length. Most baits and lures produce. Some excellent fly water.

Sacramento River: Coastal. California's largest river. Fish show in September and run through early spring. Best October and November. Boats only in lower river; boat and bank fishing upper river. Fresh roe and lures best.

Smith River: Coastal. Late steelhead run, mid-December through February. Big fish—20-pounders not uncommon. Boat and bank fishing. Winged bobber is a preferred lure, but other lures and bait also produce. Generally too high for fly fishing.

Trinity River: Klamath River tributary. Starts producing in August and continues through winter. Best months October and November, with good flurry in February. Some summer steelhead. Accessible most of its length. Yarn "glo bugs," roe, nightcrawlers and flatfish are good. Fine fly fishing at times.

OREGON

MAJOR STEELHEAD STREAMS

Alsea River	Illinois River	Santiam River
Applegate River	Imnaha River	Siletz River
Big Creek	John Day River	Siuslaw River
Chetco River	Kilchis River	Sixes River
Clackamas River	Klaskanine River	Smith River
Clatskanie River	Little Nestucca River	Snake River
Columbia River	Miami River	Tenmile Creek
Coos River	Millacoma River	Tillamook River
Coquille River	Molalla River	Trask River
Deschutes River	Necanicum River	Umatilla River
Drift Creek	Nehalem River	Umpqua River
Eagle Creek	Nestucca River	Willamette River
Elk River	Rogue River	Wilson River
Grande Ronde River	Salmon River	Winchuck River
Hood River	Sandy River	

CHASING THE STEELHEAD

Alsea River: Coastal. Fishing good November through March. Best December to February. Primarily a boat-fishing river, with bank access at a premium. Plugs and bobbers widely used.

Columbia River: Biggest river on the West Coast. Holds fish all year, but most are caught in summer because of high water conditions in winter. Best in July and August, tapering off in September. Boat fishing primarily, with bank fishing from sand and gravel bars. Tributary mouths usually good. All baits and lures used.

Deschutes River: Columbia River tributary. Prime summer-run stream July through October, best August and September. Holds fish all year, but lightly fished in winter. Boats allowed for transportation only—no fishing from them. Artificial lures used primarily. Excellent fly-fishing stream. Some sections restricted to flies only.

Nestucca River: Coastal. One of Oregon's top three steelhead streams. Good fishing all year. Winter run November through March, best December and January. Summer run peaks in June and July, with a good late flurry in September and October. Boat and bank angling in lower river, bank only in upper reaches. Highway 101 parallels most productive stretch from Beaver to Three Rivers. All baits and lures produce.

Rogue River: Coastal. No. 1 in Oregon, beginning with ½-pounders in September. Fishing holds up through March, and any of these months except March could be the year's top producer. Boat and bank fishing, some areas reached only by boat. Bait, lures, flies.

Fish on! Angler has his hands full with Deschutes River iron-head. Oregon Wildlife Commission photo.

Winter steelheaders drift fish at Three Rivers on Oregon's famed Nestucca River. Oregon Wildlife Commission photo.

Limits all 'round! Limit catch of summer steelhead from Oregon's Wilson River is displayed by Rick Doryland, Don Schomberg and Dick Martin. Don Schomberg photo.

196

Sandy River: Columbia River tributary. Good December through March, best December and January. Fishing from boats prohibited in most upper river, but boats are handy for transportation. All baits and lures are used.

Siletz River: Coastal. Holds fish all year, with winter run November through March, best late December through February. Late summer run September and October. Best summer months June and July, with boat and bank fishing. Bait and lures.

Umpqua and North Umpqua River: Coastal. One of Oregon's top three rivers and another all-year producer. Best winter months November to February, best summer months July to October. North Umpqua is a prime summer-run stream July through September. Boat or bank fishing, but parts of river cannot be fished from a boat. Also, fly-fishing-only restriction on some portions. Elsewhere, bait and lures produce well.

Wilson River: Coastal. Produces all year, with winter run November through March, best December and January. Summer run June to October, best June and July. Boat only in lower portion below Mills bridge; good bank access throughout. Bait, lures, flies.

WASHINGTON

MAJOR STEELHEAD STREAMS

Bogachiel River	Klickitat River	Skagit River
Calawah River	Lewis River	Skykomish River
Cedar River	Lyre River	Snake River
Chehalis River	Methow River	Snohomish River
Columbia River	Naselle River	Snoqualmie River
Coweeman River	Nisqually River	Soleduck River
Cowlitz River	Nooksack River	Stillaguamish River
Drano Lake	Pilchuck River	Tokul Creek
Duwamish River	Puyallup River	Toutle River
Elochoman River	Pysht River	Walla Walla River
Elwha River	Queets River	Washougal River
Grays River	Quinault River	Wenatchee River
Green River (King Co.)	Samish River	Willapa River
Hoh River	Sammamish River	Wind River
Humptulips River	Satsop River	Wynoochee River
Kalama River	Sauk River	Yakima River

Columbia River: Fished all year by Washington and Oregon anglers. Summer best due to high water in winter. Best from June through September, with July tops. Boat and bank fishing with all types lure and bait. Tributary mouths especially productive.

Cowlitz River: Columbia River tributary. Topped Skagit in 1970–71 and has been No. 1 Washington steelhead stream ever since, due to massive hatchery plants. Fishing is good all year, with best winter months November through April, tops December to February. Best summer months July and August. All fishing, boat and bank, downstream from hatchery barrier dam at Salkum. Excellent fishing immediately below salmon and trout hatcheries. All types lures and bait, some flies.

Green River (King County): Flows into Puget Sound. Washington's No. 3 steelhead stream. Winter season December through March, best December and January. Summer run developing with hatchery plants. Bank access at selected locations. Boat fishing banned most of length. Eggs, lures, flies.

Humptulips River: Coastal. December through March, best December and January. Boat or bank fishing. Most lures and baits produce.

Kalama River: Columbia River tributary. Has fish all year. Best winter months December and January. Best summer months June and July, with August and September also good. Boats used for transportation; fishing from boats prohibited most of river length. Lures, bait, flies. Flies increasingly popular for summer-runs.

Lewis River: Columbia River tributary. Good all year, with East Fork most productive. Best winter months December and January; best summer months June and July. Good boat and bank access. Bait, lures, some flies in summer.

Puyallup River: Flows into Puget Sound. Winter fishing December through March, best December and January. Primarily bank fishing.

Skagit River: Flows into Puget Sound. No. 2 Washington steelhead stream. Topnotch fishing December through April, with best months December and January. Summer run being developed with hatchery plants. Boat or bank fishing, with boats used extensively. Big river, big fish. All types bait and lures.

Skykomish River: Flows into Puget Sound. Winter fishing December through March, best December and January. Boat and bank fishing with lures and bait.

198

*Steelheader works likely-looking hole on a Western Washington River.
Washington Game Department photo.*

Scrappy steelhead tears up surface of Washington's Humptulips River.
Washington Game Department photo.

Stillaguamish River: Flows into Puget Sound. North Fork most productive. Good fishing December through March, best December and January. Summer run developing on North Fork with hatchery plants. Boat and bank fishing, with fishing from boats banned on North Fork. Bait and lures used, with flies only permitted during summer on North Fork.

Toutle River: Tributary of Cowlitz River. Produces fish all year. Winter fishing consistently good December through March. Summer fishing best June and July, but continues good through September. Excellent bank access to main river, with some boat fishing at lower end. All baits and lures used, with flies popular for summer fishing.

IDAHO

Idaho steelhead are all products of the Snake River system, and are fished in the Snake and its tributary rivers, the Clearwater and the Salmon. There are two distinct races. The "A" Group spawns in the Salmon River, and in Oregon's and Washington's Imnaha and Grande Ronde rivers. The "B" Group is native to the Clearwater and Snake.

"A" Group fish begin hitting on the lower Salmon in early October, and provide good action as far upstream as the mouth of the Pahsimeroi River near Challis. The "B" Group begins bending rods in September along the Snake, and peaks in the Snake and Clearwater in October and November.

Idaho steelheaders braved snow storm for this nice catch of "A" Group steelhead from Hell's Canyon area of Snake River. Idaho Fish & Game Department photo.

201

"B" Group fish are enormous bruisers, generally running 12 to 16 pounds, with about one out of five topping the 20-pound mark. The Idaho state record steelhead—30 pounds, 1 ounce—was taken November 22, 1973, from the Clearwater River. On the same day, the Washington state record was set when a 35-pound Clearwater-bound fish was hauled from the Snake River just north of Clarkston. Unfortunately, both these areas were flooded in 1975 by the Lower Granite Dam.

The future of steelhead fishing in the Pacific Northwest is moot. Man, the ultimate consumer, is at the same time the fish's best friend and worst enemy. Dams have inundated spawning areas, perverted stream flows, blocked spawning runs and imperiled migrating fish. Improper logging practices have spoiled many fine streams, and industrial pollution and roughshod development have taken their toll.

State and federal agencies have countered with massive, innovative hatchery programs which have breathed life back into California's American, Trinity and Sacramento rivers and augmented runs in many Oregon and Washington streams.

Oregon's Alsea, Sandy and Wilson rivers are better than ever, thanks to hatchery plants. Summer runs have been introduced in a number of rivers, and the Deschutes, North Umpqua, and Siletz owe their fine summer fishing to Oregon Wildlife Commission enhancement programs.

Steelhead fishing in Washington is twice what it was in the "good old days," thanks to Game Department hatcheries which put close to six million smolts into state waters each year. Burgeoning summer runs in the Skagit, Green, Cowlitz, Elwha, and north forks of the Lewis, Toutle and Stillaguamish rivers owe their origin to hatchery stocks.

A prodigious new U.S. Fish and Wildlife Service hatchery on the north fork of Idaho's Clearwater River is designed to produce one million "B" Group smolts a year, in mitigation for loss of spawning area corked off by the Dworshak Dam.

Despite this, there have been notable setbacks, primarily in the well-damned Columbia River system. Fishing in Washington's legendary Grande Ronde River was drastically curtailed in 1974. That same year, sportfishing was closed on the entire Snake River system in October, almost before the Idaho steelhead season began. A scant 15 percent of the expected return of "A" and "B" Group fish cleared Ice Harbor Dam, the first of four impoundments on the lower Snake River.

Cathy Campbell and Jim Bates team up to display Snake River Group "B" Steelhead that topped 20 pounds. Brad O'Connor photo.

Perhaps the most critical threat to steelhead sportfishing lies in the resolution of treaty claims by indigenous Indian tribes. In a head-on collision of progress and regression, a U.S. District Court judge ruled in March, 1974, that treaties written more than a century ago gave Indian signatories a right to more than half the anadromous fish, including steelhead, in western Washington. He further enjoined the state from any interference with this fishery.

Full implementation of this decision, and its application in other states, would leave both sportsmen and state management agencies at a severe disadvantage.

It is hoped that reason will prevail, making the steelhead fair game for all fishermen of good conscience.

Here's how to put a fish on a stringer. Wire is run through "transparent" membrane in lower jaw. Don't run stringer through both lips or through gills. Get the fish back into the water with a minimum of handling and it will stay alive.

204

Don't Spoil Your Fish

VIN T. SPARANO

If you sit down at the dinner table and bite into a poor-tasting bass or walleye fillet from a fish that you caught, there's a good chance the second-rate taste is your own fault. In all probability, the fish was not handled properly from the moment it came out of the water. Fish spoil readily unless they are kept alive or quickly killed and put on ice.

Here are the necessary steps involved in getting a fresh-caught fish from the water to the table, so that it will retain its original flavor. First, the decision to keep a fish dead or alive depends on existing conditions. If you're out on a lake and have no ice in your boat, for example, you'll want to keep all fish alive until it's time to head home. Under no circumstances should you toss fish in the bottom of the boat, let them lie there in the sun, then gather them up at the end of the day. Try that stunt and the fillets will reach your table with the consistency of mush and a flavor to match. Put your fish on a stringer as quickly as possible and get them back in the water, where they can begin to recover from the shock of being caught.

Use the safety-pin-type stringer and run the wire up through the thin almost-transparent membrane just behind the fish's lower lip. This will enable the fish to swim freely.

Do NOT shove the stringer wire under the gill cover and out of the mouth. This damages gills and kills fish fast. Also avoid cord stringers, where all fish are bunched in a clump at the end of the cord. This is perhaps acceptable on short trips for small panfish, which are generally caught in big numbers and quickly cleaned. But if you're after bigger fish and want to keep them alive and fresh, use the safety-pin stringer.

If you're rowing or trolling slowly, you can probably keep the stringer in the water. If you have a big boat and motor, however, it's a good idea to take the stringer into the boat for those fast runs to other hotspots. If the run is fairly long, wet down the fish occasionally. But don't tow a fish in the water at high speed—you'll drown it.

On a trip to Quebec, where the best walleye spot was a 3- or 4-mile run from camp, I used another technique to get fish back alive. Whenever returning to camp with a stringer of walleyes, I'd stop my boat every ½ mile or so and ease the fish over the side. I'd let the fish swim around for 5 minutes or so before hauling them back in the boat and continuing the trip to camp. During the course of a week, I made such trips several times and always reached camp with lively walleyes to be put in our shoreline fish box. Keeping fish alive is especially important on extended trips to remote areas, where ice in sufficient quantity isn't generally available.

While on the subject of lengthy fishing trips to remote areas where ice is not available, let's talk about how to keep fish alive for a week or more. I use a homemade collapsible fish box, which can be weighted with a rock in a foot of water on shore or floated in deep water. Either way, the fish will stay until the end of the trip. Keeping fish alive for lengthy periods in remote areas is impossible without such a box. Keeping fish on a stringer at dockside will NOT work for long periods. With some wood and wire mesh, a fish box is easy to build.

We're assuming, of course, that a fish has been unhooked and is placed in the fish box in good condition. If it has been deeply hooked and appears to be dying slowly, however, it's best to kill the fish immediately, gut it, and keep it on ice.

Killing a fish quickly is simple. Holding the fish upright, impale it between the eyes with the point of your knife or rap it on the head with a heavy stick. The important factor is killing it quickly, since the more slowly it dies the more rapidly the flesh will deteriorate.

If you're a stream fisherman, it's wise to carry your catch in a canvas or wicker creel. The canvas creel works fine, so long as it is occasionally

Here's Giby Russell's collapsible fish box for use on long trips where ice is not available. Floated in deep water, the box will keep a good number of fish alive during an extended trip. Note size and construction of the fish box.

Fish box need not be floated in deep water. It can be weighted with a rock along shoreline as shown, so fish can be conveniently dropped in without hauling box out of the water.

One way to kill a fish is a quick thrust between the eyes with a knife, as shown. Another method is rapping the fish on the head with a heavy stick.

The wicker creel still does its job well. Lined with wet ferns or grass, as shown here, or with wet newspapers, it will keep fish reasonably cool on the hottest days.

immersed in water. The traditional wicker creel will work just as well, but it should be lined with ferns, leaves, or wet newspaper.

If you're a surf fisherman, you can bury your catch in the damp sand. Just remember to mark the spot. A burlap sack occasionally doused in the surf also makes a practical fish bag. The important factor is to keep the fish cool and out of the sun.

Regardless of the various ways to keep fish cool, they should first be

The canvas creels are simple to use. Giby Russell dips his entire creel in a stream, wetting it thoroughly. His fish will keep in good shape during a day-long trip.

cleaned properly. With a bit of practice and a sharp knife, the job can be done in less than 1 minute. First, insert your knife, blade outward, in the anal opening of the fish and slit the skin forward and up to the gills. With the fish opened, cut and pull out the gills and entrails. Next, with the fish on its back, run your fingernail against the backbone and remove the blood sac along this area. Now wash the fish out. Try to avoid washing the inside of a fish more than once, since water directly on the flesh tends to make it soft and cuts down on flavor. Some veteran anglers simply wipe out their fish and cook it, with no washing at all.

One bit of advice for saltwater anglers: Clean your fish in either saltwater or a brine solution. Washing a saltwater fish in a brine solution will help retain the original flavor.

Surf fishermen should bury their catch in damp sand. This will keep it cool and out of the sun. Remember to mark the spot!

Vin T. Sparano with a fine catch of trout from New York waters. With good field care, the trout will reach home fresh and firm.

211

Field dressing a fish properly will literally take only seconds with some practice. First step is holding fish belly up and making a cut from anal opening up to gills.

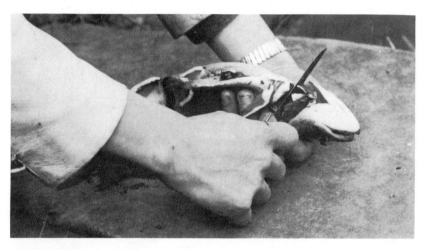

Make two cuts at gills, one below (as shown) and one above the gills where they form a V.

Next, stick finger into gullet (as shown) and begin to pull downward. Gills and entrails should come out with little trouble.

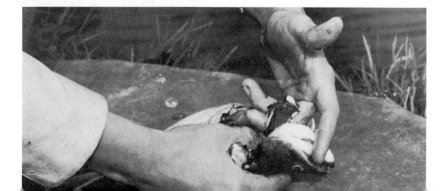

With entrails out, run your thumbnail along backbone to break and clean blood sac.

Final step is a quick wash in the stream. Washing the fish once is enough. The less water coming into direct contact with the meat the firmer the flesh will turn out.

213

Getting your fish home in good shape is as important as cleaning in producing a tasty fish dinner. Placing gutted fish on ice is not good enough. The ice will melt and the fish will soon be underwater. The flesh will absorb water and become mushy and tasteless. There is really only one way to handle the problem and that is to pack the fish in plastic bags and place the bags on ice in an ice chest.

If you don't have an ice chest, you can still work out a solution. Place the fish in one plastic bag, then place that bag in another bag full of ice. Your fish will be iced down, but not in direct contact with the ice—and you won't even need an ice chest. You can plan ahead for such situations by carrying plastic bags in your car or tackle box.

Field dressing or gutting fish is generally the accepted method with trout and species such as pike and pickerel. Most other species can be filleted, and this is the technique I use with all the fish I catch that lend themselves to this quick and easy way of producing a boneless piece of meat.

I prefer filleting for many reasons, and frequent fishing trips to Canada always seem to prove to me that filleting is the only way to go.

Carry a couple of plastic bags in your tackle box. They work out fine when an ice chest is not available. Put ice in one bag (left) and your fish in the other (right). Then place the bagged fish in the bag with the ice. Your catch will be iced but NOT *in direct contact with ice, where it would get soggy in water from melting ice.*

Don't Spoil Your Fish

On one Canadian trip, for example, three friends and I loaded our two boats for the return trip from an Ontario outpost cabin to the main lodge. We had just wrapped up a week of good fishing for smallmouth bass and walleyes in the province.

In addition to a lot of gear, the four of us were taking our possession limits of fish home to our families, and we were doing it with one medium-size cooler and some ice. How were we able to get nearly 50 bass and walleyes, plus ice, in one ice chest? Easy! We were hauling only fillets, leaving heads, fins, and innards behind for the 'coons.

Making it easier to haul fish out of the backwoods is only one reason for filleting. There are others. When putting together a shore lunch, for example, a fillet is a lot easier and faster to cook up in a skillet than a fish that is only field dressed.

Then there are the guys with fish-bone phobias, and I'm one of them. There are no bones in a fish fillet, so I fillet whenever possible. I also have small children who enjoy fish and who literally take on more than they can chew. I rest a lot easier knowing they are eating fillets that are free of bones.

Many youngsters, like Matt Sparano, can't cope with fish-bones. For these persons, learning how to fillet a fish is especially important. Using the method shown here, the fillets will be free of bones.

Also, since entrails are left intact when filleting, it is not necessary to field dress the fish. Neither is it necessary to scale the fish, since the final step of the filleting technique is skinning and the skin is discarded, scales and all.

The accompanying photographs show, step-by-step, how to fillet a fish. While it looks like a complicated job, the 5-pound largemouth bass in the photographs was actually filleted and skinned in about 4 minutes. Note that the bass was filleted with very little mess to clean up, since gutting and scaling were not necessary. This method can be used with almost all species of fish, from big saltwater striped bass to small panfish.

I want to add a word of caution here. In some regions, such as Ontario, the skin must be left on the fillet so that identification of the species can be determined by fish and game officers. If you're unsure of the law where you're fishing, check it out with local authorities or leave the skin on the fillet until you get home. Skinning a fillet literally takes only a few seconds and you'll make almost no mess in the kitchen.

With a sharp fillet knife, make two cuts, one on each side of the dorsal fin and as close as possible to the dorsal fin. The cuts should go as deep as the backbone and run lengthwise from behind the head to the tail.

216

This is how the two initial cuts should look from top of the fish.

Now make a diagonal cut, as shown, just behind the head and down to the backbone. Take care not to cut into or puncture the stomach and entrails.

Slipping the knife into one of the initial cuts made alongside the dorsal fin, begin to work the blade around the backbone and rib cage, cutting the fillet away from the body. Use the flexible blade to help you carve off a complete fillet without any waste.

Keeping the blade flat, continue to cut around rib cage and down to the belly skin.

When the meat is freed from the carcass, cut through the belly skin and separate the fillet completely from the fish. Now turn the fish over and cut away the fillet on the other side exactly the same way.

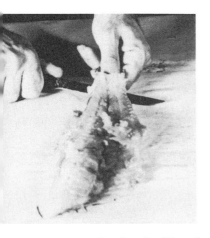 

To skin the fillet, place it flesh side up as shown here. Hold the fillet down with fingers or the tines of a fork if it is too slippery. Work the flat of the blade between meat and skin.

Using a slight sawing motion and keeping the blade flat and against the skin, work forward and separate the meat from the skin. A slightly dull knife works better for skinning than a sharp fillet knife.

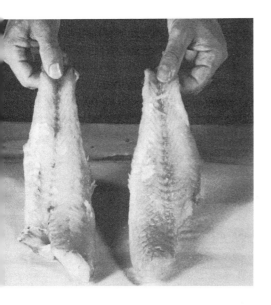

Here are the two finished fillets—completely free of bones and ready for the pan. Remember that gutting and scaling is not necessary.

Obviously, the best time to cook and eat fish is immediately after your catch is filleted, when original flavor is at its peak. This is O.K. for a shore lunch or with a small catch when you reach home, but some problems do arise when fillets cannot be eaten this soon. I use a few rough rules of thumb that work for me.

If I've caught small fish that I have not filleted, for example, I see nothing wrong with wrapping the field-dressed fish in clear plastic wrap and placing them on a platter in a refrigerator—so long as you plan to eat them within *24 hours*. Some flavor will be lost, but not enough to really be concerned about. Fillets, however, whose meat is completely devoid of skin and scales, should be eaten within *12 hours*. Ideally, they should be eaten the day you catch them.

Unfortunately, eating fresh fish fillets this quickly is not always possible and they must be frozen. Some flavor will always be lost when freezing fish, but it's a matter of degree. Do the job right and you may never notice the difference. Don't drop fillets in a plastic bag and toss them in a freezer. There will be air pockets in the bag and you're well on your way to producing a fillet loaded with freezer burn.

The ideal way to freeze fillets, or fish in any form, is in a block of ice. Any container can be pressed into service, such as milk cartons, pie plates, trays made from aluminum foil, and so on. The important factor is not to let any part of the fillet touch the surface of the container. The fillet should be completely encased in ice.

I'll be the first to admit that while this is the ideal way to freeze fish, it is not always practical, especially with small freezers. An alternative is to wrap the fillets carefully and tightly in one of the various brands of freezer paper. I prefer the clear plastic wrap because I can get nearly all the air out and prevent freezer burn. I can also see what's in the package if the label should fall off.

So long as the fillets are wrapped properly and frozen quickly, it's safe to say that lean fish, such as cod, flounder, and bass, can be kept in a freezer up to 6 months before it begins to lose quality. Fatty fish, such as tuna, bluefish, and mackerel, can be kept in a freezer up to 3 months.

If the fish is frozen in a block of ice, however, it can just about be stored indefinitely. I would not hesitate, for example, to eat a trout or walleye fillet that had been frozen in a carton of solid ice for a couple of years.

Many people also claim that you cannot safely refreeze a fish. These persons are only half right. If you take a couple of fillets out of the freezer and later change your mind about having fish for dinner, the fillets *can* be refrozen BUT ONLY IF THERE ARE STILL ICE CRYSTALS ON THE FLESH. The fillets will lose some flavor and texture, but as long as they are not completely thawed, they can be frozen for another day.

A few words should be included here about fish knives. Some anglers may be able to fillet a fish with the same sturdy sheath knife they used to dress out their buck last season, but they would be much better off with a filleting knife with a flexible blade about 4 to 6 inches long. It's also wise to carry a sharpening stone. Since you will be making initial cuts through fish scales, your blade will lose its edge rather quickly. A few strokes on a stone between cuts will make the job a lot easier. The only time a sharp knife is not necessary is during the final skinning stage. Actually, a dull knife works better, since it will not accidentally slice into the fillet.

Any discussion on the preparation of fish will invariably bring on cries of disagreement from many readers, but here's some advice based on personal experience and I'll stick to it. Here it is, short and simple: The less a fisherman tampers with fresh fish, the better it will taste. A fresh walleye fillet, for example, should not even be breaded, but simply fried until flaky. Eat it with a touch of salt and lemon juice—nothing else. The largemouth bass fillets should be floured, dipped in egg, and rolled in bread crumbs. All they require is a light browning on both sides in a frying pan with hot oil. It's pretty tough to come up with a simpler recipe that will make fish taste as good.

A trophy muskellunge from Little Bass Lake in Oneida County, Wisconsin.
Wisconsin Department of Natural Resources photo.

The Magic
of the Muskellunge

BOB CARY

The Ojibwa called him "maskinonge" which translates out something like "big ugly fish," an apt description of the biggest, meanest, smartest, and most spectacular member of the freshwater pikes. To other, smaller species unfortunate enough to inhabit the same waters, he is the devil incarnate, a malevolent aquatic terror straight from hell.

To that relatively small, highly dedicated and tightly disciplined troop of anglers who spend unaccountable hours equipping, planning and executing each waterborne assault on the muskie, he offers the sportiest piscatorial challenge extant. For that balance of the angling clan, that vast army of sport fishermen who occasionally raise and tie into a huge scissorbill while seeking bass, walleye or panfish, the muskellunge is a tackle-shattering ticket to cardiac arrest.

Once upon the sky-tinted waters of Wisconsin's big Lac Court Oreilles, my wife Lil and I were methodically probing an underwater "cabbage bed" with black bucktail-and-spinner lures. Fifty yards away, two youngsters in an anchored aluminum skiff were filling a wire basket with perch by way of tiny minnows fished with fly rods. As we drifted near them we noted a surge of water just off the stern of their craft

223

and a panic-stricken flurry of fingerling perch. Simultaneously, one red-and-white bobber dipped and went under. The boy hauled back, his rod tip nodding as a 10-inch perch yielded to the pressure. Suddenly a torpedo shape shot past the gunwale, engulfed the perch, and dived.

The youngster let out a yell and grimly gripped his arching rod while the thick line whistled through the snake guides. Momentarily, the pressure eased and he hastily stripped in slack. Then the two boys gasped. Ten feet from the boat a great fish surfaced. The sunlight glinted on 50 inches of thick silver-and-olive muskellunge.

Other than the regular opening and closing of his gills, the fish was nearly motionless. Scar tissue around his jutting underjaws testified to numerous encounters with hooks during his two decades of predatory existence. Following that mistaken rush to capture what he assumed was an injured perch and the telltale tug of the barb, he surfaced, as was his custom, to assess the situation. Usually he had found an outboard motor shaft, stringer, dangling oars or a taut anchor rope to wrap the line around. In this instance, he had a choice of all four. The anchor rope was closest.

In a tremendous shower of spray the forked, reddish caudal fin whipped upward as the muskie bunched 40 pounds of muscle and dived. The monofilament leader touched the rope and popped like thread. In seconds, the waves subsided, the lake surface flattened into glossy reflections and the two stunned boys peered unbelieving into the depths.

Lil and I cast that spot religiously for the next three days but we never saw that fish again. Nor did we learn the names of those two boys in the skiff. They are grown men, now, wherever they are, and undoubtedly that huge fish is still vivid in their eyes. In all probability, it is 12 inches longer and 20 pounds heavier by verbal campfire measurement, an acceptable and even customary aspect of muskie lore.

The incident on Court Oreilles is cited because it contains much of the essence of muskie angling: surprise, excitement, disappointment. It also points up a fact well known to muskie specialists—few real big muskies are taken by anglers seeking other fish and on tackle not designed for the heavyweights. Not to say that a fly rod or light spin stick cannot be used for the big predators. They can. In the hands of such pros as New York's legendary Len Hartman, the lightweight sticks are deadly weapons. Len set an impressive list of light line records ranging from an 18-pound 7-ounce muskie on 2-pound thread to a 67-pound 15-ounce giant on 10-pound monofilament.

However, most successful muskie specialists use sturdier equipment. Delmar, New York, angler Arthur Lawton used heavy-duty gear to subdue his current 69-pound 15-ounce world record St. Lawrence River trophy in 1957. And Rice Lake, Wisconsin, fisherman Louis Spray used a stout bait-casting outfit to bust his 69-pound 11-ounce Chippewa Flowage muskie that was once the world record and is still the state champion.

Tough bait-casting, spincast, or heavyweight spinning tackle is simply good insurance on a muskie safari . . . along with a deep, wide-rimmed landing net or gaff. At one time, .22 pistols were much in vogue for putting the quietus on an unruly monster but resort owners, particularly, heaved a sigh of relief when firearms went out of favor. Unnumbered are the stories of nervous marksmen who attempted to perforate a gyrating fish and instead shot lines, leaders, oars, gunwales, keels, tackle boxes, and even boots.

Most guides carry both net and gaff. The net is used in fish up to 25 pounds, the gaff for muskies in the saw-log category. These are as essential to his craft as a fund of good stories. And there is no other freshwater fish which has been the subject of more yarns, rumors, legends and unadulterated fiction.

None, of course, can top the 102-pound giant which was reported in the May 11, 1902, issue of the Minocqua, Wisconsin *Times,* a scaly behemoth taken along with an 80-pounder by fisheries personnel netting Minocqua and Tomahawk lakes for fertile females. Verification, however, leaves some doubt. John Klingsbiel, Superintendent of the Wisconsin fish propagation program, says: "There are always stories about those 100-pound muskies going around, but we've never seen one."

Klingsbiel's crews annually net spring-run females for hatchery spawn. They've never seen a 100-pounder, or even an 80-pounder. But that doesn't prove that such an old rod-wrecker doesn't exist.

Certainly, there is ample documentation of the unfortunate Duluth sportsman who nailed a monster in Wisconsin's Middle Eau Claire Lake and had it all cut up by a taxidermist when someone decided it should be weighed. The remains, it was verified, weighed 70 pounds—a new world record if the carcass had not been dismantled.

A captive muskie shows its barred sides.

Fisheries personnel strip spawn from a big female musky. Fish are netted in spring, stripped of eggs, and returned unharmed to the water.

226

But there are hundreds of 30-, 40- and 50-pound specimens which did get boated, weighed, and measured and now stare down in varnished splendor from countless living room walls throughout the continent. Most of these giants came from the northern areas, including Ontario, Minnesota, Wisconsin, Michigan, Ohio and New York. From its original range in the Great Lakes basin, the Mississippi River drainage, the Rainy River basin and Lake Chautauqua, New York, the fish has been spread by stocking into double its former territory.

States where muskies are found, in addition to those already mentioned, include: Georgia, Tennessee, Ohio, Pennsylvania, Virginia, West Virginia, North Carolina and Kentucky. Experimental plantings have been made in other areas, but there is no firm evidence that muskie populations have taken hold. In Canada, there is muskellunge angling in Quebec and Ontario.

New York initiated the first attempts at artificial propagation, but Wisconsin is the state which has done the most in this field. State hatcheries handle about 135,000 muskies annually for restocking, a great undertaking when it is considered that it takes about 5 pounds of minnows to raise 1 pound of muskie. Hatcheries process some 30 to 40 quarts of muskellunge eggs each spring and, at the same time, some 4,000 quarts of sucker eggs. From the standpoint of propagation, it is not the muskie that is the problem, but his food supply. From spring to fall, the fish evolve from eggs to 12-inch and even 18-inch fingerlings, and are then distributed to designated waters.

Fisheries personnel are also closely watching some experimental plantings of muskie-pike hybrids which appear to grow at twice the normal rate of pure muskies. Oddly enough, the pike by itself limits muskie production in the natural state. Where both species are present, the earlier-spawning and initially faster-growing pike quickly outstrip their brown cousins which they devour with relish. At present, artificial propagation appears the only method of maintaining catchable populations of muskies. Even under optimal conditions, this means an annual catch rate of no more than one legal muskie per acre of water per season. In most waters, it is a fraction of this.

Because the muskie is a trophy freshwater species and because it takes from 3 to 4 years for a muskie to reach 30 inches, legal length in most areas, it behooves the angler to recognize a small muskie immediately, so it can be returned promptly uninjured to the water. This quick identification is especially important in areas where there are also pike, since they can easily be mistaken for each other when small.

MUSKIE GROWTH RATES

Age	Length	Weight
1 month	1.7– 3.0 inches	—
2 months	4.1– 7.0 inches	0.3 oz.
5 months	5.8–12.3 inches	0.3– 0.5 lbs.
1 year	7.0–18.0 inches	0.3– 1.0 lbs.
3 years	16.0–30.0 inches	0.7–12.0 lbs.
5 years	18.0–41.0 inches	2.0–17.0 lbs.
10 years	32.0–52.0 inches	8.0–33.0 lbs.
15 years	45.0–57.0 inches	14.0–52.0 lbs.

(These are Wisconsin Department of Conservation growth figures and show variations for various waters with richer or poorer environment.)

The veteran muskie angler can usually tell at a glance the olive-brown, spotted, barred, or silver-sided muskie from the greenish, yellow-or-white-spotted pike. The occasional angler who thinks he may have a muskie can tell by the scales on the cheeks and gill covers. Muskies have no scales on the lower half of the cheek and none on the gill cover. The pike has small scales on the entire cheek and large scales on the gill cover's upper segment. Some biologists claim the quickest way to establish identity is to turn the fish over and count the mandibular pores, the small holes on the outside margin of the under jaw. The pike has 5 or fewer holes on each side, the muskie 6 or more.

Some places in Minnesota and Canada have a mutant form of pike which is silverish in color and can be mistaken for a muskie. This "silver pike" breeds true, seldom mixes with other pike or muskies and is usually under 10 pounds. Best advice for an angler in doubt as to what he may have on the hook, if it has a pike shape, is simply to release the fish if it does not meet the minimum size for muskies in that area.

Facing high odds, even the most skillful and best-equipped angler is well-served with another valuable commodity—LUCK. But luck, as any crapshooter knows, can be influenced to improve the odds. Perseverance is an essential asset. No real muskie fisherman ever gives up.

Even when his vacation ends and he packs his tackle to go home, he is already planning next season's assault.

At Hayward, Wisconsin, where they have the Fishing Hall of Fame and a statue of the muskie, the official state fish, there are about 50 muskie lakes. On some of these waters, the odds of getting a muskie are good. While some of the larger waters, such as the 30,000-acre Chippewa Flowage, produce more trophy fish, our preference has usually been for the smaller lakes and the East Fork of the Chippewa River. There is an excellent float on the river from the historic logging village of Shanagolden downstream to a take-out point just above Blaisdell Lake. Muskies from 6 to 10 pounds are fairly common in this stretch and an occasional 25- to 30-pounder is boated. There is also some good walleye angling interspersed among the pools, eddies and undercut banks where the Chequamegon National Forest crowds to the water's edge.

East of Hayward, along Route 77, like the productive Tiger Cat Flowage where the rumor mills have been anticipating a new world's record, and a string of fine little lakes that include Ghost, Lost Land, Moose and Teal, Lil and I fished Teal one extremely hot July day with a guide named Charley. We had agreed to meet at Ross's Resort by 6 A.M. Unfortunately, the evening before there had been a party that started at the Turk's Supper Club near town and wound up with a moonlight swim in Lac Court Oreilles. Thus it was something like 10 A.M. when we arrived at the dock, the temperature had turned the boat seats into sizzling aluminum griddles and Charley had lost his enthusiasm. "You should have been here at daybreak," he groaned. "It is too hot and still now . . . the fish won't be moving until evening."

My wife, like most women anglers, has little regard for logic. "Never mind that," she said firmly, "just get us where the muskies are and we will do the rest."

Charley gave me a hopeless glance and shrugged. We put the tackle in the boat and pushed off, Charley stroking the oars. Directly across from the dock there was an underwater gravel bar generously decorated with weeds. Charley rested on the oars, wiped sweat from his forehead and pointed his finger. "There," he said flatly.

Our muskie lures were hung in a line along the inside of the gunwale, yellow surface lures with propellers, black surface lures with metal lips, red-and-white spoons, jointed plugs, balsa minnow lures, deep-running

Bob Cary lands a Wisconsin muskie that hit in the middle of a hot July day on Teal Lake, Wisconsin.

Guide Charlie looks on as Lil Cary works hooks out of a 20-pound muskie from Teal Lake, Wisconsin.

plastic minnows, twin spinner and pork-rind lures, and black bucktail-and-spinner baits. For the flat, still surface, I selected a yellow topwater plug. Lil snapped a black bucktail into her wire leaders.

About the tenth or eleventh cast, our baits hit almost simultaneously, just inches apart. I hustled the surface lure back with the gurgling, spattering movement that the tigers prefer. Lil's bucktail-and-spinner dug in and began its slower underwater return trip, the nickel blade revolving steadily.

230

"Migod," said Charley. "There's one."

Five feet behind my noisy bait appeared the telltale "bulge" of a fish closing in just below the surface. I speeded up the retrieve and the fish speeded up. I slowed down and he slowed down. Twenty feet from the boat we saw a shadow, a swirl in the water, and he vanished. All three of us stared at the spot while I swished the lure back and forth next to the gunwale.

Suddenly about 6 feet below the oarlocks, the muskie swam leisurely past. In his mouth was a black bucktail, the spinner flickering alongside his jaw. Lil had paused in her retrieve while watching the fish chase my lure and the muskie had hit the bucktail coming at the boat.

"Set the hook!" I yelled.

"What?"

Wham. The muskie hit the end of the line with such a jolt he hooked himself and jammed the spincast reel. For some reason the monofilament held. The fish reversed, shot under the keel, hit the end of the line again, jumped twice, came back from under the boat and jumped again. With the reel jammed, Lil could only hang in and hope. If that fish had taken a straight run in any direction, he would have snapped the line, but he didn't. He circled and jumped and jumped and jumped until he slid completely exhausted into the landing net. It was no trophy, but a beautifully marked, thick-bodied specimen just under 20 pounds. That is luck.

Over on Moose Lake there was an old submarine of a fish they dubbed the "Two O'Clock Muskie." Resort owners and guides swore that the fish only fed at 1:50 P.M. and that he seldom ventured far from his home territory around Grassy Island. Estimated at 45 pounds, the old warrior had three times defeated Indiana angler Dr. Robert Gibson and ripped a lure off the line of Bill Brown from Riverside, Illinois. One quiet evening my cousin Bill Paull, from Aurora, Illinois, and I were plugging Grassy Island, but with little success. As we moved down the shore, an acquaintance of Bill's, George Perrine, also of Aurora, arrived on the scene with guide Johnny Gates. The first shot out of the box, George let out a yell as his rod doubled sharply and a fish slammed into his lure. Gates rowed for deep water while Bill and I moved over to seats on the 50-yard line . . . and the battle was on.

The muskie was tough but George was tougher and John handled the boat beautifully. Fifteen minutes elapsed before the fish came headfirst into the net. Only it wasn't the monster, it was a 25-pounder. This was a rare instance where two big fish were in the same territory. Perhaps if Bill and I had made just two more casts we might have scored on one or the other. The last I heard about the Two O'Clock Muskie, he was still shredding lines and tearing off hooks.

The Flambeau Flowage east of Park Falls, Wisconsin, is a favorite with many giant killers and gets its share of angling activity. But the North Fork of the Flambeau River, from the Flowage dam 26 miles to Park Falls, gets relatively less pressure. Veteran guide and float-trip operator Ed Robinson introduced us to the North Fork from his base at Midway. The lower half of the float contains bigger muskies but the upper portion, from the dam to Netzel's Landing, not only contains muskies, but a healthy population of smallmouth bass and walleyes. The route is interspersed with riffles, pools, and some spectacular rapids. The thickly wooded shoreline abounds with deer, beaver, waterfowl, and porcupine. Late summer and fall are best times to float, with lures good during hot weather, and sucker minnows tops later on.

Vilas County, Wisconsin, contains more muskie lakes than any comparable area in North America, something like 200. My dad's cousin Roland Cary operated a muskie resort on Fish Trap Lake for a couple of decades and was also postmaster at Boulder Junction. Roland had been involved in several hundred muskie conquests and firmly believed a world record would come from that area. Among some of the best lakes where record-size muskies have been hooked and lost by guides and anglers are: Boulder, Trout, High, Muskellunge, Squirrel, White Sand, Kawaquesaga and Big Lake, along with a host of waters to the east around Eagle River and north to big Lac Vieux Desert which straddles the Wisconsin–Michigan line along with the Cisco chain of lakes.

Sharing its muskie waters is an accepted fact of life for Michigan. Its finest muskie lake is huge St. Clair, half inside Ontario and lying between Lake Huron and Lake Erie. Probably no other angler publicized this sport fishery as much as Homer Le Blanc, guide and lure designer. The 62-pound 8-ounce state muskie record was not taken by Le Blanc, but by angler Percy Hoover. Le Blanc, however, is credited with catching more muskies than any other person in the state, possibly the nation. The balance of Michigan's muskellunge waters are mainly along the northern and western portions of the Lower Peninsula.

The Magic of the Muskellunge

Minnesota has 88 lakes and four rivers with muskie populations; 40 of these lakes and three of the rivers at times offer excellent action. The species has always taken a back seat to the official state fish—the walleye —but is getting more prominence through efforts by the Minnesota Department of Natural Resources and a dedicated group of anglers called Muskies, Inc.

According to Stan Daley, state fish production coordinator, the annual stocking program runs to about 26,000 fish in the 8- to 12-inch size plus some fry. Minnesota fish management efforts are frustrated by the large native pike populations which prey on the young muskies.

Muskies, Inc., with headquarters in St. Paul, began a dual stocking and live-release program in 1967. Plantings in Minnesota lakes have so far totaled 7,132 muskies at a cost of $2 per fish. At the same time, the group initiated live release of legal-size fish caught, with an estimated 80 percent of all muskies boated by club members now being returned back to the waters to fight again. Each year the group gathers at Battle Lake, Minnesota, for a day-long fish-out. On June 21, 1974, some 1,300 members boated and released 41 muskies in the all-day affair.

The state record, a 56-pound 8-ounce muskie, was taken from Lake of the Woods in 1931 by J. W. Collins of Baudette and the big lake still produces huge fish, although most of the action is on the Ontario side from Nestor Falls north to Kenora. Rainy River, from International Falls downstream, was once loaded with the big fish but industrial and municipal developments have reduced this sharply. The tributary Big Fork River turns up some worthwhile trophies. The Upper Mississippi River, part of the original continental range of the muskie, is a favored stretch of float water for growing numbers of anglers. Fish up to 40 pounds have been boated in the stretch below Monticello. Luremaker and float enthusiast Dan Gapen considers the Mississippi not only a very underrated muskie stream but also one of the finest bass and walleye rivers in the United States. Headwaters lakes in Itasca, Cass, Hubbard and Beltrami counties furnish the bulk of the state's trophies with Big Leech Lake near Walker probably the most famous. The state is continually experimenting with other areas and has recently introduced muskies into the perimeter of the Boundary Waters Canoe Area.

Ontario, for sheer surface area of water, has more muskie territory than any political entity in North America. Frank Schneider, an official of Muskies, Inc., and a man with muskie blood in his veins, considers

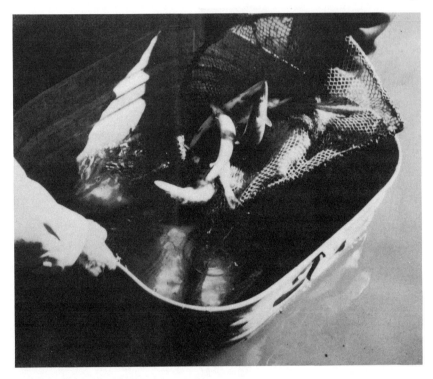

At Muskies, Inc., a private hatchery in Minnesota, it took four months to raise these 12-inch stocking-size muskies from the egg. Dr. Jerry Jurgens photo.

the northeast segment of Ontario's big Rainy Lake as excellent trophy territory. He and his friends consistently score in the over-20-pound class and swear they had an 80-pounder rip walleyes from their stringers.

Ranking at the top for many trophy hunters is Ontario's Eagle Lake, a consistent producer of giants up to 60 pounds. Resort owner Lorne MacKenzie steered me into the biggest muskie I ever came eye-to-eye with, a trophy Lil and I will never forget. This old tusker had been raised several times in a small rocky bay on the south shore of the lake, but had so far evaded capture. The first time we saw him, we were

Chetek (Wisconsin) angler Jack Iverson used a No. 5 Mepps spinner to hook this chunk muskie on Wisconsin's Potato Lake.

Canadian guide and resort owner Lorne MacKenzie shows the sizable maw on a 50-pound muskie.

Chicago angler Ed Klemme with a 50-pound muskie from Ontario's Eagle Lake.

drifting into the bay with a strong backwind, not using the motor and creating a minimum disturbance with the oars. Several loose logs were being moved around along with other flotsam by the wind and we thought he was just another partially submerged pine bole . . . until he moved.

Hastily, we cast over and ahead of him as he moved his bulk slowly across the channel outlet of the bay, but he made no move as the baits came whirling past. I let the wind carry us back to open water, then motored up the lake for a couple of hours to let him cool off. About 4 P.M. we eased back into the bay and began casting again. After about

236

a dozen casts, I lifted my bucktail from the water, swished it back and forth, then brought it up for a backcast. Five feet of solid muskie fury exploded off the stern as the fish, huge jaws agape, made a desperate grab for the bait. As he crashed down right next to the motor, Lil and I were both hit with a shower of spray. But he didn't get the hooks. A half hour of casting produced no more activity.

The next day we were back in the bay at 4 P.M. and after a few casts the big guy rolled up on top, 15 yards from the boat, eyeing us with undisguised hate. But he wouldn't hit. Finally he dived and vanished from sight. That night, in the lodge, I told Lorne about the big fish and the guests crowded around to listen. It made a great story.

The following afternoon there was a strong wind and we couldn't get across the main body of the lake to the south shore until almost 5 P.M., but we moved into the little bay and worked it carefully. Nothing happened. When we got back to the lodge we found out why. At 4 P.M., Chicago angler Ed Klemme had drifted the bay with a guide and busted that big boy on a bucktail. Klemme had his trophy hanging by the ice house. It went an even 50 pounds.

On that same trip, MacKenzie provided us with what may be the greatest muskie sport we will ever experience. With our canoe and tent, he flew us by float plane into nearby Kekekwa Lake, a narrow eight-mile-long strip of granite-rimmed water that contains nothing but muskies. To Lorne's knowledge there had never been a muskie taken over 20 pounds out of Kekekwa, but it was simply loaded with smaller ones. He had a standing arrangement that any angler who went in there did not bring any fish out. Catch what you wished, but release them.

We went in with spin tackle. Lil had bass-size gear and I took an ultralight stick with three-pound line. In two days of action we landed eight legal muskies up to 14 pounds, four more undersize, and lost probably six more fish, most of them as a result of my three-pound line getting wrapped in brush. I remember that last afternoon, tackle packed and tent rolled up while we lay stretched out on a warm rock shelf waiting for the plane to pick us up. I was watching puffs of white cloud drift across the blue Ontario sky and I thought out loud: "Lilly, the day my time is up I'm going to ask St. Peter if it's all the same with him, I'll forego the pearly gates. If I've got my druthers, he can just drop me off on the shore of Kekekwa Lake."

"Amen," said Lil.

Spring-run stripers from San Francisco Bay.

Fishing Inshore Pacific

LARRY GREEN

Inshore fishing along the Pacific Coast from Mexico north to Alaska covers an extremely wide range of ocean habitats, each of which is regulated by contributing factors such as temperature, salinity, waves, tides, shelters, and others which make up the living world for hundreds of species of marine organisms, plants, and animals.

Only after comprehending many of these complexities of such a varied total living environment can one begin to understand the existence of the numerous species of fish that share this same environment. For the fish, like the various plants and marine organisms, are vastly different in both makeup and characteristics. It is the saltwater anglers who study these differences who ultimately become the better anglers, for in each difference there is a lesson to be learned, a secret to be shared which would ultimately benefit the inshore fisherman.

STRIPED BASS

Of all the species of fish which fall under the heading of inshore fishes of the Pacific Coast, the striped bass is by far the most sought after. It is estimated that some $20 million is contributed to the economy annually by anglers who pursue the striped bass, yet, odd as it may seem, there are only two locations on the entire Pacific Coast where striped bass are caught in great numbers. One is the central coast of California, the other is the central coast of Oregon.

Originally brought to the Pacific Coast in 1879, Pacific stripers have ranged only a few miles south of their original California home, but enough fish moved up the coast to create a good fishery at both Coos Bay, Oregon, and at the mouth of the Umpqua River north of Coos Bay. Between these two main striper fisheries, however, there are not enough concentrations of striped bass to warrant mention.

The largest concentrations of striped bass still remain firmly rooted in central California's river delta areas, San Francisco, and adjoining bays, and some 25 miles of surf line adjacent to the entrance to San Francisco Bay.

At one point it was believed that California's population of adult spawning stripers had reached nearly 4 million. However, recent samplings indicate that over the past 10 years this number has been reduced to a little more than 1.5 million adult striped bass in this fishery.

Increased water needs, irrigation pumps, and industrial and sewage pollution are the assumed culprits in this alarming decline.

Despite this fact, the West still hosts some of the hottest striper fishing in the United States. The inshore waters of the Pacific Ocean and San Francisco Bay receive heavy schools of striped bass beginning in May after the bass have spawned and begun drifting down out of the river delta areas.

By June, San Francisco Bay is alive with school stripers which eventually make their way to the ocean. Once entering the Pacific Ocean the striped bass will range only a few miles up and down the surf from the mouth of the bay. The bass feed heavily on summer migrating schools of anchovies and surf smelt.

Since the stripers feed in and about the surf, they are classified as inshore fish. Surf casters and boat anglers alike get in on the action, following the birds and feeding fish up and down some 20 miles of beach.

Plugs and lures of every shape and size are used with good success, and several sportfishing boats even offer charter services to fish for striped bass in the ocean with live bait.

A thirty pounder caught by author.

Surf casting for stripers, San Francisco beaches.

By August, what began as 12-, 15-, and 20-pound school bass are now fish ranging upward of 25 to 40 pounds. Each year several fish pushing the 50-pound mark are caught from the surf of central California.

The Oregon fishery, though not as large in numbers, produces larger bass. This is a spring fishery and it is not at all uncommon to catch 50-pound-plus bass on plugs, bait, or flies in the Umpqua River fishery.

By September, most of the striped bass of central California begin migrating back into the waters of San Francisco Bay. As the baitfish in the ocean waters migrate on, the stripers return to San Francisco Bay to continue feeding on the anchovies that are in the Bay.

Fly rod striper from San Francisco Bay.

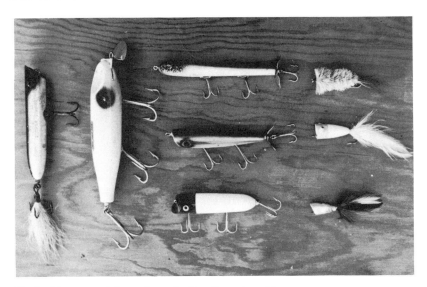

Typical lures used for stripers in San Francisco Bay.

For boat fishermen, this is said to be the best time of year to fish for stripers in San Francisco Bay. Heavy schools of stripers range throughout San Francisco and adjoining bays from the end of August through the end of October. Every man, woman, and child who fishes over the concentrated schools from a boat usually limits out. The California limit is three striped bass per rod per day of which none may be less than 16 inches in length.

Once the winter rains begin, the striped bass use the high water to make their way back up into the River Delta areas where they will lounge, pair up, and prepare for spawning again in the spring, thus completing the entire 12-month cycle.

Stripers are caught with much success throughout the winter and spring months in the rivers and deltas. However, because of usual muddy water conditions, baitfishing is the accepted rule of angling. Those river anglers who fish from boats and use big wobbling plugs also find better results if they place a strip of cut bait across the back of the lure with rubber bands. In these muddy water conditions, the fish's scent is more positive than its eyesight.

243

A pair of rock cod.

Lingcod, angler Dick Keating.

ROCKFISH

Sebastodes is a genus name for the majority of nearly 100 species of rockfish which find the inshore rocky zones of the Pacific Coast an ideal habitat to propagate.

Though found in even larger numbers and size in the deep reefs and submerged canyons offshore, these bottom-dwelling rockfish move into the shallower inshore waters to spawn during the winter and spring months. Here they will deposit and fertilize their eggs.

Rock or bottom fish are found just about anywhere along the inshore waters of the Pacific Coast so long as rocks or kelp are present. All rockfish have three similar characteristics—they are cannibalistic, spiny, and delicious eating.

The average inshore rockfish averages from 1½ to 4 pounds, whereas the average offshore deep-water rockfish averages from 3 to 8 pounds. Despite the smaller sizes, the inshore waters of the Pacific Coast abound with just about the same number of species that are found in deeper water.

244

Inshore-caught lingcod.

Of all these nearly 100 species, one bottom-dwelling fish reigns king above all others. He is the lingcod, and although the lingcod is also a deep-water fish, it is not at all uncommon to find lingcod weighing upwards of 50 pounds in less than 10 feet of inshore water. This is especially true during the months of January, February, and March when lingcod are busy spawning. Lings live a long time and one such critter just 43½ inches long proved to be nearly 17 years old.

Of all rock or bottom-dwelling fish, the lingcod is by far the top carnivore. He holds this distinction by being able to stretch his massive knife-toothed jaws over fish nearly his own size and weight. Like all rockfish, the ling is an aggressive feeder, and considering that lings have been known to reach 70 pounds, one can see why he is the prize trophy of all who fish the inshore waters of the Pacific.

Though many of the rockfish are referred to as "rock cod," they are not really the true cod which are found along the Atlantic Coast. Many of the common names of these rockfish indicate their coloring. For

245

example, there are red, blue, vermilion, yellow, brown, black, and olive rock cod.

All these rockfish are equipped with large spinning fins for quick movement when catching prey or eluding a predator. Though most are school fish, these bottom dwellers stick pretty much to one area, be it a reef, kelp bed, or other such habitat.

Though rockfish are caught primarily by boat anglers fishing inshore and offshore waters, rockfish are also taken in numbers off public breakwaters, piers, or other structures that provide some kind of protective habitat on the bottom. All cut baits, such as herring, squid, sardine, anchovies, and smelt, make an appetizing meal for most bottom fish. Natural baits, such as live fish, seaworms, shrimps, and crabs, are better yet.

Because these inshore rockfish are such aggressive feeders, a wide selection of assorted jigs tied with either feathers, hair, or yarn works well. It has been proven that red and yellow are the two best colors for rockfish, especially when these two colors are combined into one lure. If the offering wiggles, it's invitation enough for any self-respecting rockfish to slam into it.

In addition to the spiny bottom fish found everywhere along the Pacific Coast, there are a few soft-spined fish which share the same inshore habitats. Two of the most well known up and down the Pacific Coast are the green ling sea trout and the crevice kelpfish. These smoother-scaled fish are generally smaller in size than the common rockfish, but they prefer the same general habitat.

Most bottom fish are caught with rod and reel, either spinning or conventional with 12- to 30-pound monofilament line. Rockfish will avidly take lures and plugs when you can find them schooled in the shallower inshore waters.

One other finned creature bears mentioning, the common cabezone. This critter is a true member of the sculpin family of fishes. Though it rarely exceeds 15 pounds, its greenish-colored meat is considered a true delicacy to all gourmet seafood fanciers.

When you consider the 100-plus species of rockfish, plus dozens of other less significant species that could really be classified under the same general heading as rockfish, one can begin to understand just what it is that so attracts saltwater anglers to fish the inshore waters of the Pacific Coast.

PERCH

The common ocean perch, of which some 23 different species have been classified, constitutes a major portion of the inshore fishery of the entire West Coast.

These prolific spawners propagate rapidly, filling a source of fishing that is enjoyed by thousands of anglers each year. Numerous species of perch are found everywhere along the coast. Sandy beaches, rocky coves, kelp beds, piers, wharfs, breakwaters, and even open stretches of the sea provide a suitable habitat for these game little fish.

The common ocean perch feeds on a wide variety of plant and animal forms. This means that inshore bait fishermen have a wide range of baits to use in a number of various habitats. Probably more ocean perch are caught from public wharfs, piers, and breakwaters than from any other area. The reason is simple arithmetic. Perch are generally classified as school fish. The public fishing facilities usually attract schools of people as well as perch.

Though numerous species of perch have similar feeding and spawning characteristics, many of the species prefer specific habitats. For example, some species of perch seldom venture in the rocky coastal areas. The perch prefer the open sandy beaches instead of grubbing around rocks and pilings for their daily food sources.

With the exception of two rather large species of sand-dwelling perch (the redtail and barred perch), most of the perch found along the sandy beaches and rolling surf are small.

These smaller but aggressive perch usually fall under the heading of surf perches. This list includes the species commonly called shiner, dwarf, silver, white, and pink surf perch. The two exceptions mentioned—redtail perch and barred perch—are two of the largest surf perch found along the Pacific Coast. These big perch will average better than 2 pounds and often exceed 3 pounds.

The largest of all known species of Pacific perch found in inshore waters is the rubberlip perch. This species has been known to exceed 6 pounds. Rubberlips frequently are found in open ocean stretches, but most prefer a habitat of wharf pilings or rocky domains and tidal pools. During their spawning periods large schools of rubberlips school in

Fishing among kelp and rocks, inshore.

the inshore kelp beds in preparation for spawning. Because they are so large they make easy targets for skin-diving spear fishermen.

Some of the other common names for perch found in the inshore waters of the Pacific Coast are striped, rainbow, black, pile, walleye, calico, reef, and kelp perch. All perch, regardless of size, color, or shape, provide a constant source of angling pleasure.

Perch are relatively simple fish to catch because they are aggressive feeders that willingly strike a wide range of offerings. Perch are sought by the most experienced anglers as well as novice fishermen because all species of perch are quite edible. In fact, some of the larger species are sold commercially in markets.

Perch are fished for in inshore waters primarily by bait fishermen who work the beaches, rocks, wharfs, piers, and breakwaters with either conventional or spinning tackle. Natural baits such as seaworms, rock crabs, sand crabs, and live shrimp are all very fine natural baits which fishermen can collect themselves and use. Strict attention, however, should be given to the fish and game laws of each state because there are laws which protect some invertebrate animals which do constitute natural perch baits.

In addition to the natural baits, anglers use a variety of cut baits for perch. These include small pieces of squid, sardine, anchovy, prawn, and shrimp.

Though perhaps only 10 percent of the West Coast anglers fish for perch with artificial lures, those that do so with light tackle know that this is the most sporting way to take perch. Not all species of perch will hit artificial lures, but among those that do are the larger species, which makes the sport even more challenging.

Generally, light spinning tackle is used for perch in inshore waters and the best producing lures seem to be small wobblers, spinners, and spoons. The little perch strike hard and fight well on light tackle.

A smaller percentage of anglers fish for perch with artificial flies. It is a proven fact that certain species, such as barred, rainbow, striped, redtail, and walleye perch, are avid takers of artificial flies. Small streamer patterns work best on school perch, but even artificial flies which represent small marine invertebrates do well on perch when they are fished in tide pools and other habitats where smaller insect-feeding perch make their home.

In California, there are several fraternities of saltwater fly fishermen who pay special attention to the surf perches and the special artificial flies that are effective on perch.

Regardless of whether you are a bait, lure, or fly fisherman, the fact remains that on the West Coast the common ocean perch makes up a major portion of the inshore fishery.

Two other factors put the perch high on the list for inshore saltwater anglers. In addition to great numbers and range, perch can be caught all year. There are no controlled seasons on most species. Also, most all species of perch provide a unique food source. Perch are not only edible, but in fact considered by some the most delicate eating of all inshore fish.

With a range extending from the tip of Baja California, north to Alaska and with better than 23 species constituting millions of school perch, it is easy to understand why the common perch plays such an important role on the Pacific Coast.

Five-pound starries.

FLATFISH

In addition to popular gamefish like the striped bass, there are several other classifications of fish which the inshore anglers seek. Of these, the family of flatfishes is not to be ignored. Flatfish include the halibut, flounder, turbot, and sole. The largest member of this family is the Pacific halibut.

Often referred to as "barndoor" halibut, this fish would really be classified as an offshore fish except for the fact that at several points along the Pacific Coast monster halibut (barndoors) weighing upwards of 200 pounds are caught in inshore waters. Port Angeles, Washington, is a good example of this fishery. On the Washington side of the Strait of Juan de Fuca, skiff fishermen tangle with monster Pacific halibut by drift fishing and mooching with rigged baits and occasionally lures.

There are other areas along the Pacific Coast where these big barndoor halibut come in close to shore and provide a unique fishery.

250

California halibut taken inshore—California coast.

In addition to these Pacific halibut, anglers have a great deal of sport with the California halibut during the summer months. The California is a smaller halibut and reaches upwards of 60 pounds. Their range is from Magdalena Bay in Baja California, north to the Klamath River.

The southern California inshore fishermen do as well as any on the California halibut, but other than its summer spawning inshore, the halibut is really more of an offshore fish.

The starry flounder is the most plentiful of all flatfish in inshore waters. Though the starry flounders are caught year-round from Point Arguello to Alaska, it is the winter fishery that excites most inshore anglers. Beginning with the first rains, schools of starry flounder begin a massive migration from salt water to brackish water to spawn. This means that the starry flounder provides active inshore sport from about November through May. California provides the best starry flounder fishing of any Pacific state. It is worthy of noting, however, that between the states of Oregon and Washington, starry flounder migrate nearly 75 miles up the Columbia River, providing anglers with a good fishery.

So delicate is the fillet of flounder that some ½-million pounds of starry flounder have been caught annually by commercial fishermen since 1935.

Flounder are the quest of bait fishermen who find best results with various marine worms, prawns, shrimp, squid, and a wide range of other cut baits like sardine, anchovy, and herring. Flounder have also been known to attack lures, spinners, and flies on occasion.

In addition to the popular starry flounder which average from 1 to 5 pounds, a few other flatfish like soles, sand dabs, and turbots make up the small remaining portion of the inshore flatfish populations of the Pacific Coast.

WARMER WATER SPECIES

From Santa Barbara south and on down the western face of Baja California, the inshore fishing picture changes quite drastically. The primary reason is temperature, though both flora and fauna are also somewhat modified by warming ocean temperatures in the southernmost regions of the Pacific Coast.

The change in the fishery is seen mostly in free-swimming predators.

Jack mackerel—southern California.   *Jacksmelt—San Francisco Bay.*

Lures for southern California gamefish.

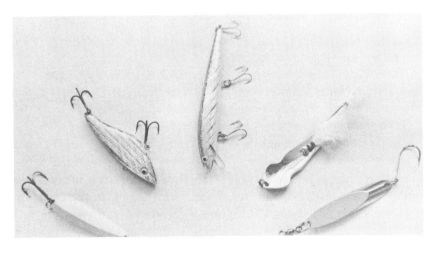

Many of the perch, flatfishes, and rockfish are found in both warm-water and cold-water climates. South of Santa Barbara, however, such predators as striped bass and salmon are a rarity.

These southerly waters play host to numerous species of swift-swimming predators that also fall under the heading of inshore fish. Among these are the bonito, mackerel, barracuda, and occasionally yellowtail. Common inshore fish, such as mackerel, bonito, and smaller barracuda are also found offshore.

Bottom fishing for rockfishes and perch in these southern warmer waters is pretty well covered under the northern sections of this chapter. The only modification may be in rigging and choice of selected baits.

The predatory fish in southern waters, however, presents inshore fishermen with a very different kind of fishing situation.

Predatory fish like the California bonito, Pacific and jack mackerel, and pencil barracuda require one common ingredient—a bait that acts very much alive. These predatory fish are not known to be avid takers of cut or even natural baits unless it is a live and free-swimming anchovy, mullet, or some other choice of wiggling bait.

The second-most accepted method is the use of lures and plugs, either cast or trolled. These predators generally school up, and part of the trick is locating the roving schools. Medium tackle, either spinning or conventional with 12- to 15-pound-test line, and a wide choice of wobbling darting lures are used.

OTHER INSHORE FISH

In addition to the numerous species of inshore fish listed here, several less significant species are also a part of the inshore fishing picture along the Pacific Coast. Among these are some 6 to 8 species of sharks and rays which are not considered very edible, yet no one who has ever caught them could say that they are not game.

Some of the smaller species not previously mentioned in this chapter include the common jacksmelt, the white croaker, and the spotfin croaker. The croakers are very common residents in bays and surfs from Magdalena Bay, Baja California to Vancouver Island, British Columbia.

Croakers get up to about 15 inches in length, but are extremely game for their size. Croakers will strike just about any offering and can

Sharks are a past-time inshore fishery.

usually be found in large schools. Their heavy iodine taste does not make the croaker the most delicate eating, but they are very game and considered top sport by many anglers.

This chapter does not provide a complete text of all species of inshore fish, but it does cover the major species in a fishery that caters to hundreds of thousands of anglers along the Pacific Coast.

Improved Clinch Knot is used to tie lures and bait hooks to lines and leaders.

Step 1—*Run end of line through the eye of the lure or hook, then make a minimum of five turns around the standing part of the line. Now run the end of the line through the opening between the eye and the start of the twists and then run it back through the large loop as shown.*

Step 2—*Pull slowly on standing part of line, taking care that the end doesn't slip back through the large loop and the knot snugs up against the eye. Trim off the end.*

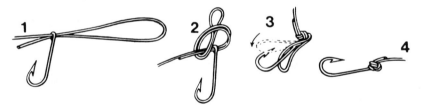

Palomar Knot (Breaking Strength 95 to 100%) is used to tie lures, hooks, and swivels to lines and leaders. It is a simpler and stronger knot than the Improved Clinch.

Step 1—*Double end of line and insert it through the eye of lure or hook.*

Step 2—*Without tightening it, tie an overhand knot with the doubled line.*

Step 3—*Holding the overhand knot, place the loop over the hook.*

Step 4—*Holding hook in one hand, pull the double end with the other hand until loop slides past the eye of the hook and tightens up against the eye.*

Step 5—*Clip off the ends and knot is complete.*

256

Knots for the Fisherman

VIN T. SPARANO

Most fishermen learn to tie a few adequate knots and let it go at that. Many use 10-pound-test monofilament and never catch a bass heavier than 3 pounds, so why should they bother? I felt the same way many years ago. Then I made my first trip to Canada and lost a muskie that looked as long as an oar. One of my "adequate knots" parted where it was tied to a wire leader. I learned how to tie good knots fast, and, if I hear about a better knot, I learn how to tie that one, too.

Tying good knots that won't slip or seriously reduce the strength of the line for a particular job is not hard. In fact, it's easier to tie a good knot than a poor one. For one thing, you won't have to waste time trying to figure out if you're using the right knot. Learn to tie the knots shown here and you'll know which is the best knot for the job.

Understandably, all knots will reduce the strength of a line and this reduction is expressed in percentages of the pound-test of the unknotted line. For example, an 80-percent knot will change 10-pound-test line into 8-pound-test at the knot. Ideally, anglers should not use knots that are rated less than 80 percent. Unfortunately, this is not always possible. There are times when we must settle for a less efficient knot simply because it is less bulky and will slip through the rod guides and tip more easily. Many good knots are rated at 90 percent and higher. A few knots, properly tied with good monofilament, will push 100 percent.

To connect my line to a lure, for example, I've always used the Improved Clinch, which is a 90- to 95-percent knot. Comparatively new, however, is the Palomar Knot, which does the same job, is easier and faster to tie, and has a rating, if properly tied, of 95- to 100-percent. This is not a great change in the line strength, but it's enough to make me start using the Palomar more frequently. The same principle applies to all other knots.

Other factors, of course, determine which knots should be used. There are three knots here, for example, that are used to connect two lines, but the knots are by no means interchangeable. The Blood Knot connects monofilament lines of equal or similar diameter; the Improved Blood Knot will join lines of greatly different diameters; and the Nail Knot is tops for tying the butt end of a leader to a fly line. Each knot has a specific job and anglers would do well to learn how and when to use them.

Don't wait until you are at streamside to tackle a new knot. The Nail Knot can sometimes be tough enough to tie properly at home. I'm not embarrassed to say that I frequently make two or three stabs at it until I'm satisfied with the finished product. Practice tying these knots until you've got them down pat. It's not a bad idea to use a rope or cord during these practice sessions. You'll learn the knots easier and faster with such heavier line.

When tying knots, bear in mind that it is important to form and tighten the knots properly. They should be tightened slowly and steadily for maximum efficiency. And when instructions require you to make turns around the standing part of the line, remember to make a minimum of five such turns.

Of the 45 or so knots that I have seen and tied, I have selected the ones most important to me. I recommend them to all fishermen who want to strengthen that link between themselves and trophy fish. Remember the old adage about the chain being as strong as its weakest link? In this case, it's the knot.

Here's a list of breaking strength percentages for most of the basic knots.

Name of Knot	Pound Test of Line	Percent of Unknotted Line Strength Using Regular Du Pont Monofilament*
Improved Clinch Knot	6-lb.	95–100%
	12-lb.	90–95%
	20-lb.	90–95%
Improved Clinch Knot using double strand	6-lb.	90–95%
	12-lb.	90–95%
Improved Clinch Knot with double loop thru eye	6-lb.	90–95%
Blood Knot	6-lb. tied to 6-lb.	90–95%
	12-lb. tied to 12-lb.	90–95%
	20-lb. tied to 6-lb.	90–95%
	20-lb. tied to 20-lb.	90–95%
Stu Apte or Double Strand Blood Knot	6-lb. tied to 20-lb.	90–95%
	12-lb. tied to 40-lb.	90–95%
Surgeon's Knot	6-lb. tied to 20-lb.	95–100%
	12-lb. tied to 40-lb.	95–100%
Improved End Loop Knot	6-lb.	70–75%
	12-lb.	70–75%
Perfection Loop Knot	6-lb.	60–65%
	12-lb.	60–65%
Turle Knot	6-lb. tied to No. 8 Hook	55–60%
Lark's Head Knot	6-lb.	75–80%
Tucked Sheet Bend Knot	6-lb.	50–55%
Dropper Loop Knot	6-lb.	65–70%
Overhand or Wind Knot	6-lb.	45–50%
	12-lb.	45–50%
	20-lb.	40–45%
Terminal Tackle Knot	12-lb.	95–100%
	20-lb.	90–95%
Bimini Twist Knot	12-lb. (wet)	95–100%

* This data was derived from tying 10 knots for each type knot and size line evaluated—a total of more than 500 knots tested. *Courtesy of the Du Pont Company.*

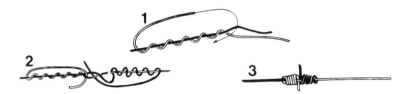

Blood Knot (Breaking Strength 90 to 95%) is used to connect two lines of the same or similar diameters. This is an especially useful knot in making tapered fly leaders.

Step 1—*Wrap one strand around the other at least five times and run end into the fork as shown.*

Step 2—*Make the same number of turns, in the opposite direction, with the second strand. Run its end through the opening in the middle of the knot, in the direction opposite that of the first strand. Now hold both ends together so that they cannot slip (try using your teeth here). Next pull the standing part of both strands in opposite directions, tightening the knot.*

Step 3—*Tighten securely and trim off both ends. The knot is complete. If you want to tie on a dropper fly, leave one of these ends about 8 inches long.*

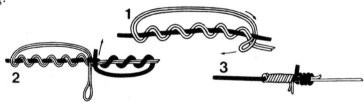

Improved Blood Knot (Breaking Strength 90 to 95%) is excellent for joining two lines of greatly different diameter, such as a heavy monofilament shock leader and a light leader tippet.

Step 1—*Double a length of the lighter line, wrap it around the standing part of the heavier line at least five times, and run the end of the doubled line into the "fork" as shown.*

Step 2—*Wrap the heavier line around the standing part of the doubled lighter line three times, in the opposite direction, and run the end of the heavier line into the opening, in the direction opposite that of the doubled line.*

Step 3—*Holding the two ends to keep them from slipping, pull the standing parts of the two lines in opposite directions. Tighten the knot, using fingernails to push the loops together if necessary. Clip off the ends.*

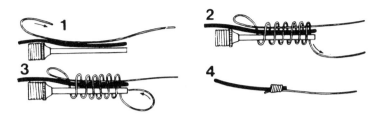

The Nail Knot is the best knot for joining the end of a fly line with the butt end of a fly leader. The completed knot is streamlined and will run smoothly through the guides of a fly rod. The Nail Knot, as its name implies, is generally tied with the use of a nail. I have found, however, that the knot is much more easily tied when using an air-inflation needle of the type used to inflate basketballs and footballs. The tip of the needle must be cut or filed off so that the tube is open at both ends. A large hypodermic needle with its point snipped off also works well. In tying Step 3, the butt end of the leader—after having been wrapped five or six times around the fly line, leader, and tube—is simply run back through the tube (needle). Then the knot is tightened, the tube removed, and the final tightening is done.

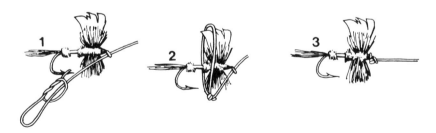

The Double Turle Knot is used to tie a dry or wet fly to a leader tippet. It is not as strong as the Improved Clinch Knot, but it allows a dry fly's hackle points to sit high on the water.

Step 1—*Run the end of your leader through the eye from the front and tie a slip knot, wrapping the end around twice, as shown.*

Step 2—*Snug up the loop and pass it over the fly, from the rear.*

Step 3—*Slowly and steadily pull the loop tight, making sure it wraps around the head of the fly.*

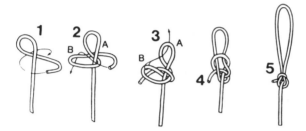

Perfection Loop Knot (Breaking Strength 60 to 65%) is used to make a loop in the end of line or leader.

Step 1—*Make one turn around the line and hold the crossing point with thumb and forefinger.*

Step 2—*Make a second turn around the crossing point, and bring the end around and between loops A and B.*

Step 3—*Run loop B through loop A.*

Step 4—*Pull upward on loop B.*

Step 5—*Tighten the knot.*

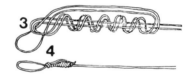

End Loop (Breaking Strength 70 to 75%) is used to form a loop in the end of a line.

Buffer Loop is used to attach lure to line or leader with a nonslip loop.

Step 1—*Tie simple overhand knot in line, leaving loop loose and leaving end long enough to complete the knot, and then run end through eye of lure.*

Step 2—*Run end back through loose loop, and make another overhand knot, using end and standing part of line. Tighten overhand knot nearest to lure eye, and then tighten second overhand knot, which, in effect, forms a half-hitch against first knot.*

Step 3—*Finished knot.*

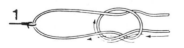
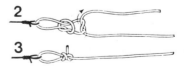

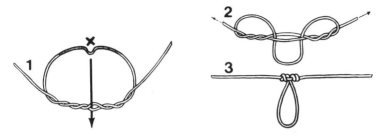

The Dropper Loop Knot (Breaking Strength 65 to 70%) is frequently used by fishermen for putting a loop in the middle of a strand of monofilament.

Step 1—*Make a loop in the line and wrap one end overhand several times around the other part of the line. Pinch a small loop at point marked X and thrust it between the turns as shown by the arrow.*

Step 2—*Place your finger through the loop to keep it from pulling out again, and pull on both ends of the line.*

Step 3—*The knot will draw up like this.*

Snelling a Hook

Step 1—*Cut leader material about 4 inches longer than length you'll need when the snell is completed. Run one end through the eye, as shown, so it extends along the shank about as far as the turn and barb.*

Step 2—*Run the other leader end through the eye in the opposite direction, letting it extend a couple of inches beyond the eye. (continued)*

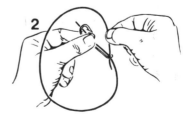

263

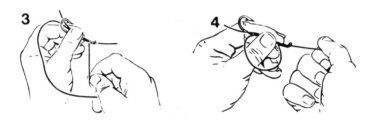

Step 3—*Holding the two pieces of leader along the shank with thumb and finger of the left hand, take a leg of the loop which hangs down from the eye and wind a tight coil around the shank and the leader ends you're holding. Wind from the eye toward the hook.*

Step 4—*After 10 to 15 turns around the shank, hold the tight coil in place with fingers of the left hand. Grasp the leader end protruding from the eye and pull steadily until entire leader has passed under the coil and tightened it on the shank. Use pliers to pull the leader end extending toward the hook up tight. Clip off this end flush.*

Attaching Hook or Lure to Leader Wire. Used to prevent sharp-toothed fish from biting through terminal line. Use No. 9 or No. 10 leader wire to practice this tie.

Step 1—*Run about 4 inches of the end of the leader wire through the eye of the hook, lure, or swivel, and then bend end across standing part of the wire. Holding the two parts of the wire at their crossing point, bend the wire around itself, using hard, even, twisting motions.*

Step 2—*Both wire parts should be twisted equally.*

Step 3—*Then, using the end of the wire, make about 10 tight wraps around the standing part of the wire. Break off or clip end of wire close to the last wrap so that there is no sharp end, and job is complete.*

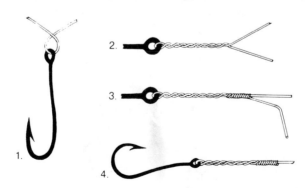

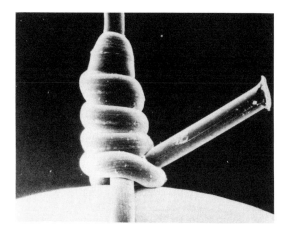

Here's an Improved Clinch Knot, photographed at 60 times natural size through a scanning electron microscope. The knot is tied with 2-pound-test "Stren" fluorescent monofilament fishing line, into the eye of a No. 12 hook. This shows how the prescribed five turns cushion the line and protect against breakage in the knot. Photo Credit: The Du Pont Company

This is a Palomar knot, tied with 2-pound-test "Stren" fluorescent monofilament fishing line onto the eye of a No. 12 hook and enlarged 60 times through a scanning electron microscope. Note how the loop of doubled line cushions the tension and protects against breakage in the knot. Tests show this knot will hold up to 95 to 100 percent of the unknotted line strength. Easier and quicker to tie, it is as strong as the popular Improved Clinch Knot. Photo Credit: The Du Pont Company

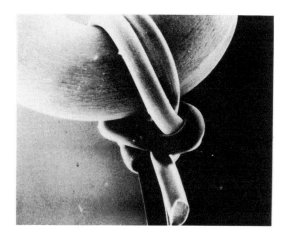

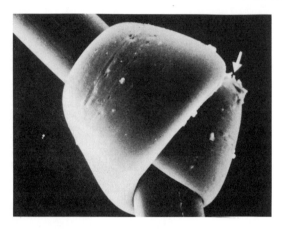

Here's why an overhand is the most destructive knot a fisherman can tie in monofilament line. This photo, taken through a scanning electron microscope, shows what happens when stress of only about 60 percent of the pound-test rating is placed on an overhand knot tied in 2-pound-test line. Arrow shows fracture of the line extending above the knot where cutting action occurs, causing it to break. The magnification is 200 times actual line size. Photo Credit: The Du Pont Company

The Bimini Twist is used to create a loop or double line without appreciably weakening the breaking strength of the line. Especially popular in bluewater fishing for large saltwater fish, this knot requires practice.

Step 1—*Double the end of the line to form a loop, leaving yourself plenty of line to work with. Run the loop around a fixed object such as a cleat or the butt end of a rod, or have a partner hold the loop and keep it open. Make 20 twists in the line, keeping the turns tight and the line taut.*

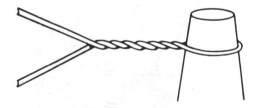

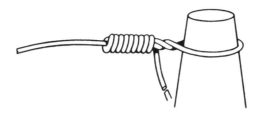

Step 2—*Keeping the twists tight, wrap the end of the line back over the twists until you reach the V of the loop, making the wraps tight and snug up against one another.*

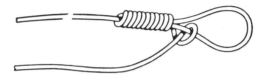

Step 3—*Make a half-hitch around one side of the loop, and pull it tight.*

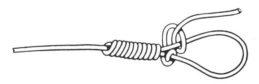

Step 4—*Then make a half-hitch around the other side of the loop and pull this one tight.*

Step 5—*Now make a half-hitch around the base of the loop, tighten it, clip off excess line at the end, and the Bimini Twist is complete.*

267

*Spider Hitch is another knot that serves the same function as the Bimini
Twist to create a double line with the full strength of an unknotted line. The
Spider Hitch is as strong as the Bimini Twist. It has been tested at from
98 to 100 percent of the unknotted line strength.*

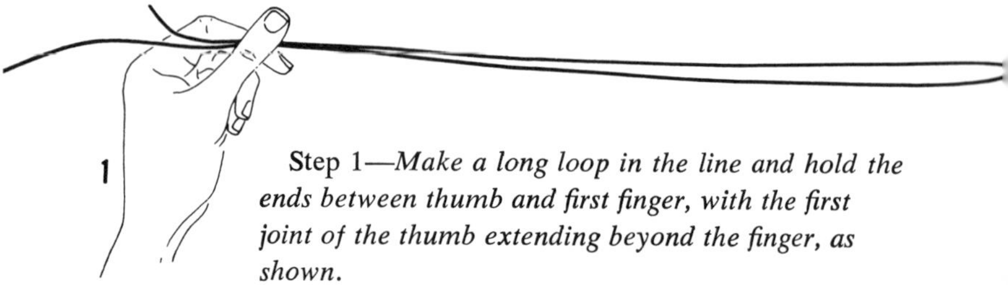

1

Step 1—*Make a long loop in the line and hold the
ends between thumb and first finger, with the first
joint of the thumb extending beyond the finger, as
shown.*

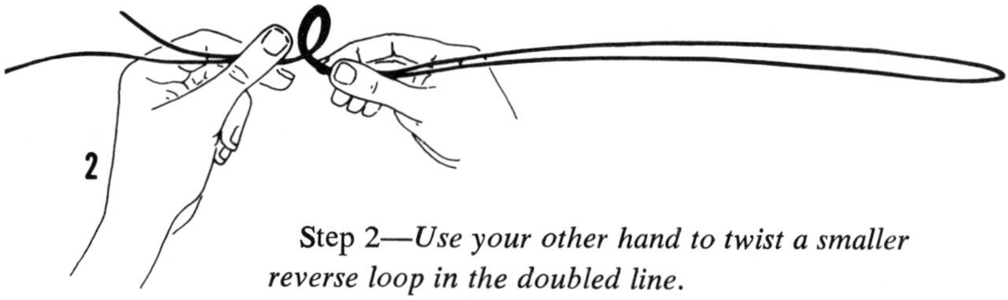

2

Step 2—*Use your other hand to twist a smaller
reverse loop in the doubled line.*

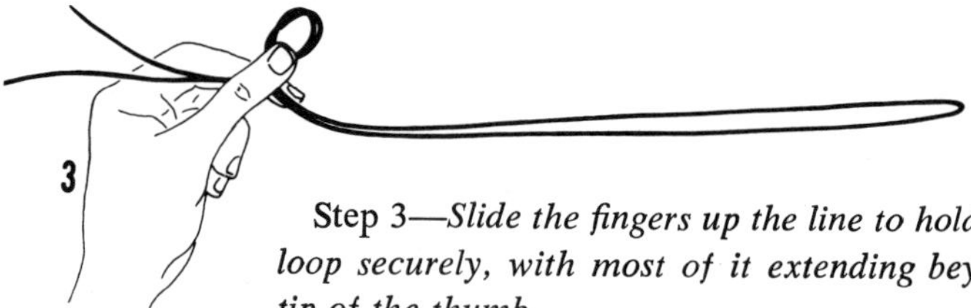

3

Step 3—*Slide the fingers up the line to hold the
loop securely, with most of it extending beyond the
tip of the thumb.*

Step 4—*Wind the line from right to left around both the thumb and the loop, taking five turns. Then pass what remains of the large loop through the small one.*

Step 5—*Pull the large loop to make the five turns unwind off the thumb. Use a fast, steady pull—not a quick jerk.*

Step 6—*Pull the turns around the base of the loop up tight and snip off the protruding end of the line.*

For Further Reading

ARNOV, B., *Fishing for Everyone*, Hawthorne Books, Inc.

BATES, J. D., *Atlantic Salmon Flies & Fishing*, Stackpole Books.

BATES, J. D., JR., *Streamer Fly Tying & Fishing*, Stackpole Books.

BATES, J. D., JR.; HALL, BAIRD; MARSHALL, MEL; RICE, F. PHILIP; SOSIN, MARK, *Tacklebox Library*, Outdoor Life-Harper & Row.

BERGMAN, RAY, *Trout*, Alfred A. Knopf.

BLADES, WILLIAM F., *Fishing Flies and Fly Tying*, Stackpole Books.

BLAISDELL, HAROLD F., *Tricks That Take Fish*, Henry Holt & Company.

BROOKS, JOE, *Complete Book of Fly Fishing*, Outdoor Life-A. S. Barnes & Company, Inc.

————, *Complete Guide to Fishing Across North America*, Outdoor Life-Harper & Row.

————, *Complete Illustrated Guide to Casting*, Doubleday & Company.

————, *Trout Fishing*, Outdoor Life-Harper & Row.

BROOKS, JOSEPH W., JR., *Salt Water Fly Fishing*, G. P. Putnam's Sons.

COKER, ROBERT E., *Streams, Lakes, Ponds*, University of N.C. Press.

DALRYMPLE, BYRON, *Sportsman's Guide To Game Fish*, Outdoor Life-Harper & Row.

EVANOFF, VLAD, *How To Fish in Salt Water*, A. S. Barnes & Company, Inc.

————, *How to Make Fishing Lures*, Ronald Press Company.

————, *1001 Fishing Tips & Tricks*, Harper & Row.

FARRINGTON, S. KIP, JR., *Fishing the Pacific*, Coward-McCann, Inc.

FENNELLY, JOHN F., *Steelhead Paradise*, Mitchell Press Limited.

FLICK, ART, *New Streamside Guide*, G. P. Putnam's Sons.

GABRIELSON, IRA N., *The New Fisherman's Encyclopedia*, Stackpole Books.

270

For Further Reading

GRESHAM, GRITS, *Complete Book of Bass Fishing,* Outdoor Life-Harper & Row.

HAIG-BROWN, RODERICK, L., *Return to the River,* William Morrow & Company.

HERTER, GEORGE L., *Professional Fly Tying & Tackle Making,* Herter's, Waseca, Minnesota.

HEWITT, EDWARD R., *A Trout & Salmon Fisherman for Seventy-Five Years,* Abercrombie & Fitch & University Microfilms, Inc.

HIDY, VERNON S., *Sports Illustrated Book of Fly Fishing,* J. B. Lippincott Company.

LABRANCHE, GEORGE M. L., *The Salmon & the Dry Fly,* Arno Press.

LUCAS, J., *Lucas On Bass Fishing,* Mead & Company.

LYMAN, HENRY; WOOLNER, FRANK, *Complete Book of Striped Bass Fishing,* A. S. Barnes & Company, Inc.

MARINARO, VINCENT C., *A Modern Dry Fly Code,* Crown Publishers, Inc.

MARSHALL, ARTHUR R., *A Survey of the Snook Fishery of Florida,* University of Miami Press.

McCLANE, A. J., *Standard Fishing Encyclopedia,* Holt, Rinehart & Winston, Inc.

McNALLY, T., *Fisherman's Bible,* Follett Publishing Company.

MIGDALSKI, EDWARD C., *Fresh Water Sport Fishes,* The Ronald Press Company.

NEEDHAM, PAUL R., *Trout Streams,* Winchester Press.

NETBOY, ANTHONY, *The Atlantic Salmon, A Vanishing Species,* Faber & Faber.

PARSONS, P. ALLEN, *Complete Book of Fresh Water Fishing,* Outdoor Life.

QUICK, JIM, *Fishing the Nymph,* The Ronald Press Company.

REINFELDER, A., *Bait Tail Fishing.* A. S. Barnes & Company, Inc.

RICE, F. PHILIP, *America's Favorite Fishing,* Outdoor Life-Harper & Row.

ROSKO, M., *Fishing from Boats,* Macmillan Company.

————, *Secrets of Striped Bass Fishing,* Macmillan Company.

SCHARFF, R., *Esquire's Book Of Fishing,* Harper & Row.

SCHWIEBERT, ERNEST G., JR., *Matching The Hatch,* Macmillan, Ltd.

SHAW, HELEN, *Fly Tying,* The Ronald Press Company.

SKUES, G. E. M., *Nymph Fishing for Chalk Stream Trout,* Adam & Charles Black.

SWISHER, DOUG; RICHARDS, CARL, *Selective Trout,* Crown Publishers, Inc.

WALDEN, H. T., *Familiar Freshwater Fishes of America,* Harper & Row.

WALKER, C. F., *The Art of Chalk Stream Fishing.* Stackpole Books.

WATERMAN, CHARLES F., *Modern Fresh & Salt Water Fishing,* Winchester Press.

WULFF, LEE, *The Atlantic Salmon,* A. S. Barnes & Company, Inc.

Index

INDEX

INDEX

INDEX